LEONHART LOWELL LAPONNEL

Get Rich The New Way

20 Steps to Wealth and Abundance in the New Era

First published by Lucidism - Motivatrz LLC 2024

Copyright © 2024 by Leonhart Lowell Laponnel

All rights reserved. No part of this publication may be reproduced, stored or transmitted in any form or by any means, electronic, mechanical, photocopying, recording, scanning, or otherwise without written permission from the publisher. It is illegal to copy this book, post it to a website, or distribute it by any other means without permission.

Leonhart Lowell Laponnel asserts the moral right to be identified as the author of this work.

Designations used by companies to distinguish their products are often claimed as trademarks. All brand names and product names used in this book and on its cover are trade names, service marks, trademarks and registered trademarks of their respective owners. The publishers and the book are not associated with any product or vendor mentioned in this book. None of the companies referenced within the book have endorsed the book.

Disclaimer

This book has utilized AI as a writing aid, supporting research, editing, and proofreading. While AI tools have contributed to refining the content, all ideas, concepts, and perspectives remain those of the author, Leonhart Lowell Laponnel.

Cover art has been created in Midjourney by author.

First edition

This book was professionally typeset on Reedsy.
Find out more at reedsy.com

Contents

Introduction: The Dawn of a New Wealth Paradigm — v
Chapter 1: Breaking the Chains - Understanding the Great... — 1
Chapter 2: Chaos as Your Ally - Turning Uncertainty into... — 5
Chapter 3: Beyond Money - Redefining Abundance — 9
Chapter 4: Consciousness Shapes Cash - The Quantum Nature of... — 14
Chapter 5: Cultivating Intuition - Your Inner Compass to... — 18
Chapter 6: Upgrade Your Mindset - Reprogramming Scarcity... — 23
Chapter 7: Energy Management - The New Time Management — 29
Chapter 8: Authentic Value Creation - The Alchemy of Turning... — 34
Chapter 9: The Zen of Money - Balancing Attachment and... — 39
Chapter 10: Prosperity Through Collaboration - From... — 44
Chapter 11: Emotional Wealth - Transforming Financial... — 49
Chapter 12: Creative Income Streams - Unlocking Your Inner... — 54
Chapter 13: Ethical Wealth Building - Prosperity with... — 60
Chapter 14: Aligning with Universal Cycles - Timing Your... — 65
Chapter 15: Sustainable Wealth Practices - Building Lasting... — 70
Chapter 16: Generosity as a Wealth Accelerator - The Power... — 75
Chapter 17: The Creative Economy - Abundance Through... — 80
Chapter 18: Financial Resilience - Weathering Economic... — 85
Chapter 19: Aligning Wealth with Purpose - Prosperity as a... — 90
Chapter 20: Generational Wealth - Leaving a Legacy — 95
Conclusion: Claiming Your Birthright of Abundance — 100

Thank you for reading this book   106
About the Author   108

Introduction: The Dawn of a New Wealth Paradigm

Try to see yourself standing at the edge of two very different worlds. One of them is familiar and built on the old ideas of wealth we've been taught to chase our entire lives. It's a world where success is measured in money, assets, titles, and competition. It's the story of climbing a ladder, often by stepping over others, with the only reward being a higher rung. It's a model that's worked for some, but for many, it has led to burnout, emptiness, and a sense of never really having "enough."

But there's also another world right before you, just waiting for you to take a step forward. This world belongs to the new Aquarian Age. This isn't just an astrological buzzword or the title of a '60s song. It's a paradigm shift we are standing on the brink of. A new way of thinking, being, and understanding what true wealth looks like. This shift is not about leaving money behind or ignoring financial stability. It's about redefining what wealth really means. It's about expanding your definition to include freedom, health, connection, joy, and the kind of abundance that makes life worth living.

The old way of wealth mainly focused on the external: cash, assets, and competition. It was all about accumulating as much as possible, often at the cost of personal well-being or community. The Aquarian Age is about flipping that model inside out. It's about internal wealth. It's about how rich your experience is, how deep your relationships go, and how true you are to your purpose. The real currency here is consciousness. Imagine measuring your success not by the size of your bank account but by the quality of your life.

To make this shift more relatable, let's take a look at James. James is a mid-level executive at a big firm. He's spent the last two decades working 60-hour weeks, meticulously saving, and climbing the corporate ladder. He's got the nice car, the respectable title, and the kind of salary that makes people nod approvingly at dinner parties. But James feels a void inside. The more he accumulates, the more restless he becomes. He's exhausted, his relationships are shallow, and he still fears losing it all despite the promotions. His version of wealth feels like a castle built on sand—one economic storm could bring it all crashing down.

James represents many of us. We've been sold on a version of wealth that doesn't nourish us. We're told to chase more, but "more" never fills the gap.

The new Aquarian Age invites us to step out of this cycle. It tells us that real wealth is multidimensional. It's about having financial resources but also having time to enjoy them. It's about emotional richness, meaningful connections, and contributing to something bigger than yourself.

This shift isn't just a personal transformation; it's also a collective one. The old wealth paradigm thrived on competition—the idea that for one person to win, someone else has to lose. But look around the world today: collaboration is becoming the key to success. Communities thrive when they share resources and create together rather than compete against one another. This is the essence of Aquarian wealth—an interconnected prosperity where everyone's growth supports the growth of others.

Think about the internet. It's a perfect example of this new kind of wealth. It's built on the idea of sharing information. One person's blog post can inspire someone across the globe. A shared video can spark a movement. Knowledge is abundant, and sharing it only makes it grow. In the Aquarian Age, wealth is like that, too. It's not finite. It's not a pie where one slice taken means less for everyone else. It's more like a flame that lights other candles—each flame grows, and the room gets brighter.

And this doesn't mean financial wealth is irrelevant. Money is still necessary. It's just no longer the only measure of success we have. It's a tool, not the goal. In the Aquarian model, money flows as a byproduct of living in alignment with your purpose and values.

You see it like this: you had to chase money in the old paradigm. In the new paradigm, you become the kind of person that money naturally gravitates towards. You attract prosperity because you're creating value, not just trying to extract it from others.

There's an important distinction here between the hustle culture of the past and the empowered creation of the present. Hustle culture taught us to work harder, grind longer, and sacrifice everything for the bottom line. It glorified exhaustion and stress as a badge of honor. The Aquarian Age invites us to work differently—to recognize that our energy is our most valuable resource, and how we use it determines our quality of life. It's about managing your energy to operate at your best rather than depleting yourself for short-term gains.

For a moment, let's return to James. What if James decided to make a shift? What if he defined wealth not by how much he owned but by how fulfilled he felt? He might decide to cut back on his work hours, taking a pay cut to regain his evenings and weekends. He could start pursuing the hobby he's neglected for years—photography. Maybe James will start an online group, sharing his photos and connecting with others who share his passion. Eventually, he even makes some side income selling prints and doing freelance work. His overall income might be lower than before, but James feels richer. His days are filled with creativity and connection, and his stress levels drop as he realizes that wealth isn't just a number in a bank account.

This story is just one example of how redefining wealth can transform our lives. The path to true abundance begins when we let go of narrow definitions of success. It requires us to question our inherited beliefs, such as "money is the only real wealth" or "success means working harder than everyone else." These beliefs have kept us locked in cycles of stress and scarcity, even when we have enough. The Aquarian Age invites us to replace these with new beliefs: that we can thrive by being ourselves, that joy and fulfillment are just as valuable as money, and that collaboration creates more wealth than competition ever could.

Try to think of a world where people define wealth as time with family, the freedom to express their creativity, and the ability to support their community. Imagine a world where success doesn't come at the cost of others' failure but is instead part of a rising tide that lifts everyone. This is the vision of the Aquarian Age—a world where our individual prosperity is tied to collective well-being. In this new paradigm, wealth is something that multiplies when shared, like love or knowledge.

To make this shift, we need to start with our mindset. Wealth is as much about perception as it is about reality. If you see the world as scarce, you'll act in ways that create scarcity—hoarding, fearing, and competing. But if you see the world as abundant, you'll look for opportunities, share, and collaborate. Your consciousness, your awareness, becomes the lens through which wealth appears.

This is what it means to say that consciousness is the new currency. It's not just about thinking positively; it's about seeing opportunities, acting on them, and being open to new ways of creating value.

This book will guide you through twenty steps to align with this new wealth paradigm. Each chapter is designed to help you shift your thinking, build new habits, and transform how you approach wealth—financially, spiritually, emotionally, and relationally. We'll explore everything from reprogramming limiting beliefs to practical ways of creating multiple income streams aligned with your passions. You'll learn how to manage your time and energy, cultivate intuition as a wealth tool, and build prosperity in ways that uplift yourself and those around you.

Think of this journey as learning to surf. The waves are already here. The chaos, change, and opportunities are all around us. You can continue to fight against them, trying to cling to the old ways and get crushed by them, or you can learn to ride them with grace and joy. The Aquarian Age is here whether we like it or not. The only question is: are you ready to step into a new way of being wealthy?

The old paradigm taught us to fear change, to see it as a threat to our security. But in this new era, change is the doorway to your abundance. The wave carries us to shores we couldn't have imagined while stuck in the safe but stifling harbors of the past. This book guides you to catching that wave—stepping into the new wealth paradigm with courage, creativity, and consciousness.

Welcome to the journey. Let's redefine what it means to be genuinely wealthy together.

Chapter 1: Breaking the Chains - Understanding the Great Shift

For a long time, we have been told a singular story about wealth. It was about the hustle, the grind, the competition. It was about climbing the corporate ladder, accumulating as much as possible, and securing your position at all costs. But as we look around today, it's clear that this model is beginning to fail – and fail quickly. The cracks are showing. More and more people are realizing that the old wealth paradigm, rooted in relentless competition and material accumulation, isn't working—at least not if we want to be genuinely fulfilled.

The world is marked by rapid technological shifts, economic upheavals, and societal transformations. The systems that were designed to create security now feel unstable and unreliable. The 9-to-5 grind that promised a safe retirement is no longer any guarantee. Investments that seemed secure can turn volatile overnight. For many, the promise of climbing the corporate ladder has led to burnout rather than bliss. This collapse of the old model, as unsettling as it is, creates space for something new. A significant shift is happening, and an opportunity to redefine wealth comes with it.

So, what is this shift I am talking about? At its core, it's a transition from focusing solely on the external—money, titles, possessions—to instead concentrating on the internal: our awareness, relationships, and sense of purpose. Wealth is no longer just about what you have;

it's about who you are and how you feel. It's about waking up in the morning with energy and excitement. It's about feeling connected—to yourself, others, and something larger than you. In the Aquarian Age, wealth is multidimensional. It includes money and emotional richness, time freedom, creative expression, and deep, meaningful connections.

This is where the idea of consciousness as currency comes into play. In the old model, wealth was a numbers game: how much could you accumulate before you retired? In the new model, consciousness is just as crucial as financial acumen. Your awareness—your ability to see opportunities, connect the dots, and understand your purpose—becomes a form of currency that enriches every area of your life. It's about being aware of the stories you tell yourself about money and recognizing which of those stories are holding you back.

Take, for instance, the quote by Rumi: "The wound is the place where the Light enters you."

This is not just a beautiful line of poetry; it's a profound truth about wealth and personal growth. Many of us carry money-related wounds—failures, losses, and fears. Maybe you lost a job and felt like a failure. Perhaps an investment went south, and you felt ashamed. These moments, these financial wounds, are opportunities. They're places where new understanding, new consciousness, can enter. The pain of losing a job might push you to pursue the passion you've been putting off finally. The fear of scarcity might lead you to discover a new way of managing money that aligns more with who you are.

In this new wealth paradigm, setbacks are not the end but the beginning of a transformation. They are invitations to grow, shift perspective, and redefine what wealth really means to you. When we see our struggles through the lens of growth, they become stepping stones rather than stumbling blocks. The Aquarian Age is not about avoiding pain or failure; it's about using every experience—good or bad—as fuel for growth and expansion.

This shift in understanding is powerful because it puts you back in the driver's seat. The old wealth model made us feel we were at the mercy of external forces—economies, markets, corporations. The new model reminds us that true wealth starts internally. It's shaped by how we think, respond to challenges, and choose to show up in the world. When you realize that consciousness is your most valuable asset, everything changes. You begin to see opportunities where others see obstacles. You start to value connection, creativity, and well-being as much as you value your bank balance.

Think about the most financially successful people you know. Chances are that their wealth didn't come just from working harder or longer than everyone else. It came from their ability to see opportunities, take risks, and trust their intuition. It came from their mindset—their consciousness. They weren't just playing the game; they were redefining the rules. This is what the Aquarian Age asks of us now: to stop playing by the old rules that limit us and to start using our awareness to create something new.

Shifting from external accumulation to internal alignment doesn't mean giving up on financial prosperity. It means expanding our definition of wealth to include what truly matters. It means recognizing that money is just one piece of the puzzle—and that without internal wealth, external wealth is ultimately unfulfilling. By breaking free from the old chains—the belief that money is the only measure of success—we open ourselves to a richer, more expansive life experience.

Exercise: Reflecting on Financial Setbacks

Take a moment to reflect on a financial setback you've experienced in your life. It could be a job loss, a failed investment, or a period of financial struggle. Write down what happened and how it made you feel at the time. Then, ask yourself:

- What lessons did this experience teach me?
- What opportunities arose from this challenge?
- How did it shape who I am today?

Write these reflections down, and notice how shifting your perspective changes your feelings about the experience.

Remember, every setback is an opportunity for growth. The wound is the place where the Light enters you. By understanding and embracing this truth, you can begin to break the chains of the old wealth paradigm and step into a new, more empowered way of being.

Chapter 2: Chaos as Your Ally - Turning Uncertainty into Opportunity

We've been taught to fear chaos. When things become unpredictable, we tense up, resist, and try to control what we can. But what if chaos isn't something to fear? What if it's an ally—a force that opens doors and creates opportunities we could never have imagined in a controlled, predictable world?

Chaos is a catalyst. It breaks down old structures, shakes us out of our comfort zones, and forces us to look at things differently. Think about times of economic upheaval. When the 2008 financial crisis hit, many people faced uncertainty. Some lost jobs, others lost investments. It was undoubtedly a challenging time. But totally new opportunities emerged for those who could handle and see through the chaos. Entire industries changed, and new ones were born. The gig economy exploded, creating flexible work opportunities that didn't exist before. People began rethinking their careers, their goals, and even their relationships with money.

Consider the COVID-19 pandemic. It brought unprecedented chaos to the world, disrupting every aspect of our lives. Yet, amidst the uncertainty, people adapted. Entrepreneurs found new ways to serve their communities. Businesses pivoted to online models, expanded home delivery services, and created new products and solutions. People who saw the chaos as an opportunity could innovate, adapt, and thrive.

The key is to understand that chaos is like a wild river. If you fall into the water, you have two choices: you can panic and try to fight against it – and probably drown, or you can accept it and let the river take you downstream – and slowly swim to one of the sides. The most significant opportunities come from learning to master the unpredictable, not resisting it. Just like a sailboat uses the wind's energy to move forward, we can use the energy of chaotic times to move towards new possibilities.

Sun Tzu once said, "In the midst of chaos, there is also opportunity." This quote holds a powerful truth. Chaos has a way of dissolving the old and making space for the new. It disrupts the status quo and forces us to re-evaluate what's important. It can lead to personal and professional breakthroughs that wouldn't have been possible in the comfort of stability.

Take Sarah, for example. She was working a corporate job she didn't love, but it paid the bills and offered stability. Then, during a period of corporate downsizing, Sarah lost her job. It felt like her world was collapsing—like the chaos was too much to handle. But with time, she began to see it differently. She used the severance pay as a cushion to start a small business—something she'd always dreamed of but never dared to pursue. The chaos forced her out of her comfort zone, and she created a life far more aligned with her true passions.

The lesson here is simple: chaos is not the enemy. It's the raw material for transformation. It's uncomfortable, yes. It's unpredictable. But it's also rich with possibilities. The most successful people are not those who avoid chaos but those who learn to dance with it. They see uncertainty not as a threat but as an invitation to grow, innovate, and explore new paths.

Think about your own life. Can you remember a time when chaos forced you to make a change? Maybe it was an unexpected move, a breakup, or a financial challenge. At the moment, it might have felt like everything was falling apart. But looking back, can you see how that chaos opened new doors? Maybe it led you to a new job, city, or even a new understanding of yourself.

The Aquarian Age will be full of chaos—economic shifts, technological advancements, disruptions of old markets, and changing social structures. Instead of fearing these waves, we must learn to ride them. When you start to see chaos as an ally, you see opportunities where others see obstacles. You trust in your ability to adapt and thrive, no matter how unpredictable things get.

Consider the story of Marcus, an independent contractor whose business was heavily affected by the sudden economic downturn. Contracts dried up, and his income plummeted. At first, the uncertainty was overwhelming. But Marcus chose not to dwell on what was lost. Instead, he focused on what he could do differently. He began diversifying his skills by taking online courses about digital marketing and consulting. Before long, Marcus pivoted his business model to include remote consulting work. This new direction provided stability during uncertain times. It opened up an entirely new set of opportunities that Marcus hadn't previously considered.

The truth is that chaos is a great teacher. It teaches us to be flexible, to let go of the things that no longer serve us, and to innovate. Our ability to adapt will define our success in a world that is changing faster than ever. Chaos asks us to stop clinging to old patterns and instead trust that we can navigate whatever comes our way. It requires us to cultivate resilience—to bounce back and grow stronger in the process.

Another analogy that's fitting here is the concept of pruning in gardening. If you've ever seen a well-pruned tree or plant, you know it looks bare and perhaps even vulnerable after being cut back. But pruning is essential for growth. The plant has to let go of old branches to make room for new growth. In much the same way, chaos prunes away what's no longer working in our lives, allowing us to grow in ways we couldn't if we were weighed down by the past.

The chaos of the Aquarian Age is not to be feared. It's here to help us evolve, question old structures, and break free from outdated definitions of success. It's here to challenge us to redefine wealth, not just in financial terms but also in terms of freedom, creativity, and purpose. By seeing chaos as an ally, we empower ourselves to transform uncertainty into opportunities for growth and greater alignment with who we truly are.

Exercise: Finding Opportunities in Chaos

Take a moment to reflect on three situations in your life where chaos led to unexpected opportunities. Write them down. What happened? How did the uncertainty force you to grow or adapt? What positive outcomes emerged from those situations? As you write, notice how chaos has often been a force for transformation, even when it didn't feel that way at the time.

Remember, in the midst of chaos, there is also tremendous opportunity. When you learn to see chaos as an ally rather than an enemy, you unlock a powerful key to thrive in the ever-changing waves of the Aquarian Age.

Chapter 3: Beyond Money - Redefining Abundance

When most people think of wealth, they think of money. Bank accounts, assets, and investments are the traditional markers of success. But real wealth is so much more than a number on a statement. It's about the quality of your relationships, the health of your body, the peace of your mind, and the joy in your heart. True abundance goes beyond the financial; it extends into every corner of your life.

Imagine for a moment that you're standing in front of two doors. Behind Door 1 is what we've been taught to value: traditional wealth. It's filled with cash, property, stocks—everything representing financial security. It's impressive, no doubt, but it's also solitary. It's a locked vault, protecting its treasures from the world.

Now, behind Door 2 lies something different. This door opens into a vibrant garden. It's overflowing with love, creativity, health, and freedom. There are people here, friends and family, sharing stories, creating art, and laughing together. It's not just about having resources; it's about experiencing life fully in every dimension.

We've been told to chase what's behind Door 1 for most of our lives. We've been conditioned to see wealth as material, something to be hoarded and protected. But in the Aquarian Age, we realize that what lies behind Door 2 is the real treasure. Holistic abundance—wealth that includes emotional fulfillment, meaningful relationships, spiritual depth, and creative freedom—truly enriches our lives.

Think about the people you admire most. Are they the ones with the biggest bank accounts, or do they seem to live fully—those who have strong relationships, are passionate, and exude joy? The truth is, you can have millions of dollars and still feel empty. You can have a huge house but no one to share it with. You can have a prestigious job title but no sense of purpose. Money, on its own, cannot fill our deeper needs.

True abundance is about integration. It's about having financial security and spending time with the people you love. It's about creating work that matters, not just because it pays well but because it feels aligned with your values. It's about taking care of your body to enjoy the fruits of your labor. It's about having the freedom to explore, be creative, and contribute to the world in a meaningful way. The Aquarian Age challenges us to step through Door 2 and redefine what it means to be truly wealthy.

Consider the story of Thomas, a high-level executive who spent years chasing financial success. He worked tirelessly, and by all traditional standards, he was wealthy. He had a luxury car, a big house, and an impressive retirement portfolio. But Thomas was exhausted. His health was declining, his marriage was strained, and he barely saw his children. One day, a health scare forced Thomas to reassess his life. He realized that despite all his accumulated money, he felt poor in the areas that mattered most. He decided to make a dramatic change.

Thomas cut back on his work hours, prioritized his health, and spent more time with his family. He also began practicing meditation and rekindled his love for painting, a hobby he had abandoned years ago. Financially, he was still secure, but more importantly, he began to feel rich in his relationships, creativity, and inner peace.

Thus, he moved from Door 1 to Door 2—from a life focused solely on material wealth to embracing true abundance in every form.

The quote, "The real measure of your wealth is how much you'd be

CHAPTER 3: BEYOND MONEY - REDEFINING ABUNDANCE

worth if you lost all your money," speaks directly to this idea. Imagine if, overnight, all your financial wealth disappeared. What would you have left? Would you still feel wealthy in other areas of your life? Would you have strong relationships, good health, and a sense of purpose? Would you still feel joy and fulfillment? True abundance aims to ensure that, even if financial circumstances change, your wealth—your inner richness—remains intact.

Let's explore the components of holistic abundance further. Emotional wealth is one of true prosperity's most important yet often overlooked aspects. It's about your ability to feel a full range of emotions, to experience joy and love, to handle challenges with resilience, and to form deep connections with others. It's about having a rich inner world where you're comfortable with yourself and can find peace even in times of turmoil. Emotional wealth makes the ups and downs of life more manageable and makes your successes feel even more rewarding.

Relational wealth is another crucial aspect. This is about the people in your life—the friends, family, mentors, and loved ones who support you, inspire you, and share your journey. No amount of money can replace the warmth of a loving family or the joy of genuine friendship. These relationships are what give life depth and meaning. They are the people who celebrate with you in good times and stand by you in hard times. Relational wealth is about nurturing these connections, making time for the people who matter, and being present in your relationships.

Spiritual wealth, on the other hand, is about your sense of purpose and connection to something greater than yourself. It doesn't necessarily mean following a particular religion; it's more about feeling connected—to nature, the universe, and your inner wisdom. Spiritual wealth provides a sense of grounding and purpose. It's what helps you navigate through the uncertainties of life with grace and trust. When you are spiritually wealthy, you feel a sense of belonging and meaning that goes beyond the material.

And then there's creative wealth—the ability to express yourself, explore, innovate, and create something meaningful. Creativity is not just for artists or musicians; it's a fundamental part of being human. It's the drive to solve problems, think outside the box, and make something beautiful or valuable. Creative wealth is about allowing yourself the freedom to explore your passions, take risks, and see the world through curious eyes. When we engage in creative pursuits, we tap into a source of joy and vitality that enriches our entire lives.

When we redefine abundance to include emotional, relational, spiritual, and creative dimensions, we open ourselves to a much richer life experience. Financial wealth becomes just one part of the puzzle rather than the entire picture. We begin to see that real prosperity is about balance. It's about cultivating richness in every area to remain resilient and fulfilled even if one aspect of life is challenged.

Exercise: Identifying Areas of Abundance

Take a moment to reflect on three non-financial areas in your life where you feel truly "rich." It could be your relationships, a passion or skill that brings you joy, or a sense of inner peace you've cultivated. Write these down. What makes you feel abundant in these areas? How do they enrich your life?

By focusing on these areas, you'll start to understand that true wealth is not just about numbers; it's about the depth and quality of your experiences. The more you nurture these aspects of your life, the more you'll begin to experience true abundance beyond what's behind Door 1.

The Aquarian Age invites us to step boldly through Door 2. To redefine wealth in a way that includes all that makes life beautiful—relationships, creativity, health, and joy. It's time to look beyond the vault and explore the garden, to see abundance as a holistic, vibrant, and deeply fulfilling

CHAPTER 3: BEYOND MONEY - REDEFINING ABUNDANCE

experience that touches every part of our lives.

Chapter 4: Consciousness Shapes Cash - The Quantum Nature of Wealth

Have you ever heard of the observer effect in quantum physics? It's the idea that observing something can change its behavior. In experiments, particles have been shown to behave differently depending on whether or not they're being observed. This strange and fascinating concept has left physicists scratching their heads for decades. But beyond the laboratory, this idea holds a powerful metaphor for our lives, especially regarding our wealth.

The observer effect suggests that our perception influences reality. In much the same way as we perceive, money and abundance shape our financial reality. If you see the world through a lens of scarcity, you'll likely experience a life where money is always just out of reach. But if you change your perception—seeing the world as abundant and noticing opportunities instead of obstacles—your financial reality begins to shift. Consciousness shapes cash. Your mindset and beliefs are the invisible forces determining your wealth experience.

Take the story of Carla, for example. Carla had always struggled with money. She grew up in a tight household, and the message she internalized was that money was hard to come by, something to be fought for and hoarded. As an adult, Carla worked long hours and constantly worried about making ends meet. Her mindset was rooted in scarcity. Every unexpected expense felt like a crisis; no matter how

CHAPTER 4: CONSCIOUSNESS SHAPES CASH - THE QUANTUM NATURE OF...

much she earned, it never seemed enough.

One day, Carla decided she was tired of feeling anxious and exhausted. She started reading about the power of mindset and how our thoughts shape our reality. Slowly, she began to change her internal narrative. Instead of focusing on what she lacked, she began to focus on what she had. She practiced gratitude, listing the things she was thankful for each day. She started noticing opportunities—ways she could use her skills to earn extra income and make connections to further her career. The more she shifted her consciousness from scarcity to abundance, the more her financial situation improved.

Carla found that by changing her mindset, she began to attract new opportunities. She received a job promotion partly because her newfound confidence made her more proactive and visible. She started a side business offering freelance services, which she had always wanted to do but was too afraid to try. As her mindset shifted, so did her reality. What had once seemed impossible—financial stability, even prosperity—was now her lived experience.

Henry Ford once said, "Whether you think you can or you think you can't—you're right." This quote perfectly captures the quantum nature of wealth. Your thoughts and beliefs act like magnets, attracting experiences that match their frequency. If you believe that wealth is something only a lucky few can attain, that will likely be your reality. But suppose you think that abundance is available to you, that there are opportunities everywhere. In that case, you begin to see and seize those opportunities.

It's essential to recognize that this isn't about wishful thinking or simply repeating affirmations in the mirror. It's about genuinely shifting your consciousness. It's about noticing your thoughts and choosing to reframe them. It's about catching yourself when you fall into patterns of scarcity and choosing a different narrative. It's about aligning your actions with the belief that you can create wealth and deserve abundance.

The observer effect teaches us that our attention is powerful. What you focus on grows. If you focus on lack, debt, and what's missing, you'll continue to see that. But if you focus on abundance—on the opportunities, connections, and resources you have—you'll start seeing more of those things in your life. It's not magic; it's the power of perception. Your consciousness shapes your cash flow.

Let's take another analogy. Imagine your consciousness as a flashlight. In a dark room filled with both treasures and obstacles, the beam of your flashlight represents your focus. If you shine it only on the challenges, you'll be surrounded by barriers and blockages. But the room suddenly looks different if you choose to shine it on the treasures and opportunities. The treasures were always there—you just needed to shift your focus to see them. The same is true for wealth. Opportunities for prosperity are often right in front of us. Still, our focus, our consciousness, determines whether or not we see them.

The quantum nature of wealth invites us to be conscious observers of our own lives. It asks us to become aware of our thoughts and understand that our mindset is not just a passive reflection of our circumstances but an active creator of them. If you want to change your financial reality, change your mind. Start by becoming aware of your thoughts about money. Are they thoughts of fear, scarcity, and lack? Or are they thoughts of possibility, abundance, and gratitude?

It's also about action. Shifting your consciousness changes your perception, but it also changes how you act. When you see opportunities, you're more likely to take them. When you believe in abundance, you're more likely to invest in yourself, take risks, and trust that things will work out. Your actions align with your new beliefs, creating a positive feedback loop that brings wealth into your life.

Exercise: Reframing Money Thoughts

Take some time to observe your thoughts about money. Write down any recurring negative thoughts you have—things like "I'll never have enough," "Money is hard to come by," or "I'm not good with money."

Once you have a list, take each thought and reframe it positively. For example, you could reframe "I'll never have enough" to "I am capable of creating abundance in my life." Reframe "Money is hard to come by" to "Opportunities to earn are everywhere, and I am open to them."

Spend a few minutes daily repeating these new, positive thoughts to yourself. Notice how it feels to shift your consciousness from scarcity to abundance. Over time, as your mindset shifts, watch how your reality begins to shift as well. Remember, consciousness shapes cash. Your perception is the key to unlocking a new experience of wealth.

The quantum nature of wealth is not about denying the challenges of the material world. It's about understanding that your consciousness is a powerful force that shapes how you experience those challenges and what you create from them. By shifting your thoughts, you change your reality. It all starts with the observer—you.

Chapter 5: Cultivating Intuition - Your Inner Compass to Wealth

Albert Einstein once said, "The intuitive mind is a sacred gift." That simple truth often gets lost in the shuffle of spreadsheets, profit margins, and financial forecasts. In our quest for wealth, we tend to idolize logic and mathematics. We think wealth comes down to knowing the formulas and playing the game right. But if that were entirely true, the richest among us would all be mathematicians and economists. They aren't. Instead, many are artists of a different kind—they are masters at trusting the intangible whispers of their intuition.

Intuition is a tricky thing. It's like that friend who never texts back but shows up right when you need them most. It's in the pit of your stomach when a deal feels wrong, or you get an electric surge of excitement about a new idea. Most people choose to ignore that feeling. Society and school have conditioned us to lean on what we can prove and see, not what we can sense and feel. But in this new Aquarian age, wealth isn't just a game of numbers—it's a dance between head and heart. Intuition is your partner in that dance, helping you spin through decisions that pure logic alone might stumble over.

Think about the great entrepreneurs of our time—Steve Jobs, Elon Musk, and Oprah Winfrey. They didn't just read the market; they felt it. Jobs trusted his gut when he decided to make the iPhone, at a time when most people couldn't see why a computer company should dive

CHAPTER 5: CULTIVATING INTUITION - YOUR INNER COMPASS TO...

into the phone business. Oprah trusted her intuition when she shifted her show to a more personal and vulnerable format, risking her career in favor of authenticity. Despite countless skeptics, Musk trusted his vision and gut to keep going with electric cars and space travel. None of these moves were strictly logical then; they were leaps of faith grounded in a deep knowing.

Before you think, "Well, I'm no Steve Jobs," remember that intuition is not some mystical power exclusive to visionaries. It's your birthright, and you've used it countless times already. Have you ever avoided a street for no apparent reason, only to find out later there was a massive traffic jam? Have you ever had a hunch about someone—a feeling you just couldn't shake—that turned out to be true? That's intuition. It's not grand and doesn't always announce itself with fanfare and fireworks. But it's there. And the more we listen and train it, the clearer it becomes.

Imagine standing at a literal fork in the road during a hike. On the left, there's a well-trodden path, wide and comfortable. On the right, a narrow trail barely visible through the thick underbrush. Logic would tell you to go left—it's safer, it's familiar, and plenty of others have done it. But there's something about the right path that stirs your curiosity. Maybe it's the scent of wildflowers wafting in your direction, or perhaps it's just the thrill of the unknown. Your gut says, "Go right."

So you do. You brush past the branches and step over the rocks. And then, after walking for a while, you come across an incredible clearing—an untouched, quiet, and beautiful place that no guidebook mentioned. That moment when you feel a sense of discovery and wonder is what happens when you trust your intuition. The world's wealth—in any sense—doesn't just live along well-trodden paths.

Let's discuss why cultivating this inner compass matters so much in pursuing wealth. For one, intuition can save you from what I like to call the "bad deal vortex." You know that situation where all the logical signs point to a "good investment." Still, something—some tiny voice inside—tells you otherwise. Ignoring that voice can cost you. Just ask anyone who's ever invested in a company that seemed flawless on paper, only for it to nosedive because of some unquantifiable, intangible flaw no one saw coming. Intuition might not spell out why it's guiding you a certain way, but it often knows what your conscious mind cannot yet comprehend.

But intuition isn't just about avoiding danger. It's also about seizing opportunities. Imagine you meet someone at a casual dinner party who's working on a project that lights you up. Logically, there's no reason to get involved—maybe it's a bit risky or out of your current line of work. But something in your gut tells you to keep that connection alive. You do, and it ends up starting an incredibly lucrative partnership. Intuition often nudges you toward those unexplored opportunities that your conscious brain hasn't fully connected yet.

To cultivate intuition, you need to be willing to make mistakes. Society likes to tell us that mistakes are signs of failure, but they're just signposts along the way. Each mistake sharpens your intuition. Each time you listen to your gut—even if it doesn't work out perfectly—you learn to hear its language more clearly. It's like learning to play an instrument. At first, every note might sound a little off – mildly said. But with practice, you start to make music. Intuition is your inner soundtrack, and every wrong note you hit brings you closer to harmony.

One powerful way to cultivate your intuition is through silence. Our world is loud. We're constantly bombarded by social media feeds, news, and unsolicited advice from every corner. To hear your intuition, you need to quiet the noise. Take a few minutes every day—maybe it's during your morning coffee or your commute—and just sit in silence. Ask yourself questions about your financial path, and then listen. It might not be a booming voice or a clear answer; it could be just a subtle feeling. Trust that feeling.

Another exercise is to make small decisions based purely on intuition.

CHAPTER 5: CULTIVATING INTUITION - YOUR INNER COMPASS TO...

Start with something low-stakes—like choosing which book to read next or what to cook for dinner. Let your intuition guide you, without second-guessing it. The more you use it, the stronger it gets. You don't need to start with life-altering choices; intuition, like any muscle, gets stronger with regular exercise, no matter how small.

Remember, intuition is also about alignment. When your actions are aligned with your true desires, intuition tends to flow more easily. If you're constantly chasing wealth in ways that feel wrong for you— if you're pursuing ventures solely because they seem lucrative, even though they don't resonate with who you are—your intuition might struggle to cut through. Wealth in the Aquarian age isn't about accumulation for its own sake. It's about freedom, creativity, and joy. When your goals align with those principles, intuition becomes a natural guide.

Consider this: the wealthiest people aren't just rich in money. They're rich in experiences, relationships, and time. They make decisions that bring them joy and fulfillment, not just cash. Wealth is a holistic concept, and intuition helps us tap into opportunities that nourish our whole selves, not just our bank accounts. When you learn to trust your inner compass, you aren't just making smart financial decisions—you're making life decisions that bring abundance in every sense.

Exercise: Trust Your Gut

Today, I want you to practice making one small decision based purely on your intuition. It could be as simple as which route to take on your way home, what to eat for lunch, or whether to contact a particular person. Pay attention to how the decision feels, not just the outcome.

Also, spend five minutes in silence today—without distractions—and ask yourself one crucial question about your financial journey. How do you feel about your current path? Don't analyze it; just feel it.

Trust the first answer that comes to you, even if it doesn't make sense immediately.

Your intuition is your sacred gift. It's that compass inside you, always pointing toward the most abundant version of your life. And in a world that often makes us feel powerless, listening to that inner voice is the most powerful thing you can do.

Chapter 6: Upgrade Your Mindset - Reprogramming Scarcity Beliefs

Buddha once said, "What you think, you become." If there's one statement that encapsulates the key to wealth in this new Aquarian age, it's this. The power of the mind isn't a cheesy concept that is reserved for motivational seminars. It's the underlying engine behind every financial decision you make, whether you realize it or not. And, just like any engine, it can be tuned for optimal performance—or it can be upgraded entirely - as we're about to discuss.

    Think of your mindset as a computer's operating system. For many of us, that mental software is running an outdated version—let's call it Scarcity 1.0. Scarcity 1.0 has bugs, glitches, and, quite frankly, some pretty terrible code. It runs scripts like "Money is hard to come by," "I can't afford that," and "There isn't enough to go around." It gets stuck in loops of fear and comparison, always focused on what you lack rather than what you have or what you could create. It's time for a much-needed update—let's upgrade to Abundance 2.0.

Scarcity Mindset: The Self-Fulfilling Prophecy

Scarcity isn't just a lack of money; it's a mindset that infiltrates every aspect of your life. It whispers that opportunities are finite, that success is reserved for a select few, and that your slice of the pie is destined to be small. Ironically, these thoughts keep you poor—even if you have money in the bank. You can have a million dollars, but if you're operating on Scarcity 1.0, you will always fear losing it, or you'll make choices based on holding on rather than expanding. Scarcity tells you, "Play it safe. Don't risk it. You don't deserve more." And over time, that mindset keeps you stuck in cycles of financial stress.

Let's use a metaphor: Imagine you're trying to fill a bathtub, but a plug is missing. No matter how much water you pour in, it just drains out the bottom. A scarcity mindset is like that missing plug. You can bring in wealth—you can get raises, earn good money, even win the lottery—but it keeps draining away, and you always feel empty. To plug the drain, you need to upgrade your belief system. Scarcity 1.0 is faulty software that perpetually tells you the tub will never be full. It runs on fear. Abundance 2.0, on the other hand, understands that there is more than enough water for everyone—and once that belief takes root, the drain seals itself.

Reprogramming with Affirmations

One of the most effective ways to upgrade from Scarcity 1.0 is to rewrite the code using affirmations. You can also find guided meditations in the bonus section at the end of this book. Now, before you roll your eyes and think, "Yeah, yeah, positive thinking," let me remind you—this isn't about forcing yourself to be happy. It's about literally rewriting your mental script. The thoughts you repeat to yourself become the beliefs

CHAPTER 6: UPGRADE YOUR MINDSET - REPROGRAMMING SCARCITY...

you live by, and those beliefs shape your actions. Think of affirmations as lines of code. Repeating them lets you enter new commands into your mental operating system.

If Scarcity 1.0 tells you, "I'm not worthy of wealth," Abundance 2.0 says, "I deserve financial freedom." If the old code says, "Money is hard to come by," the new script reads, "Money flows to me easily and frequently." These aren't magic spells—they're mental updates that slowly begin to change how you see the world and your place in it. When you install new code, your system behaves differently. And the best part is, it doesn't require grand ceremonies—just your willingness to repent, believe, and upgrade.

Visualizations: Creating Mental Reality

Affirmations are just the first step. Another powerful technique for reprogramming your mindset is visualization. Imagine you are a sculptor, and your life is the block of marble in front of you. Visualization is the act of seeing the masterpiece in your mind before you start chiseling away. Abundance 2.0 runs on visualization—it's about mentally rehearsing what you want before it becomes reality.

Picture yourself already wealthy. But don't just picture stacks of money; see the lifestyle you want. Visualize how you spend your days, how it feels to wake up without financial worry, and how your relationships evolve when you are living with an abundance mentality. This practice isn't wishful thinking; it's coding. When you consistently visualize abundance, you begin to make decisions that align with that reality. Opportunities that match your vision start appearing—not because the universe suddenly "grants your wish," but because you're finally attuned to see them.

Visualization is the upgrade that changes how you interact with the world. If you think of scarcity, you'll see closed doors, risks, and limits. If you believe in abundance, you'll see open doors, opportunities, and potential. Your mental filter dictates how you perceive reality. By visualizing your life in its abundant form, you're training your filter to see the world differently—and act differently.

Self-Hypnosis: Going Deeper into Reprogramming

Self-hypnosis might sound a bit intimidating, but really, it's just a tool for getting your conscious mind out of the way so that you can work directly with your subconscious—where your scarcity beliefs are stored. You can think of self-hypnosis as putting your mental operating system into "edit mode." During a hypnotic state, your mind is more open to suggestions, and that's when you can input new, more empowering beliefs.

It doesn't have to be complicated. You can find guided self-hypnosis sessions in the bonus section of this book. You can also find many online, focusing specifically on releasing scarcity and building abundance. All it requires is a willingness to relax and listen. You're essentially running a deep scan on your old Scarcity 1.0 code, deleting bugs, and reinstalling fresh software.

The key to self-hypnosis is consistency. You wouldn't expect a single gym session to build muscle. Similarly, one hypnosis session isn't going to completely overwrite a lifetime of scarcity programming. But with each session, you are slowly rewriting your story, one line of code at a time.

CHAPTER 6: UPGRADE YOUR MINDSET - REPROGRAMMING SCARCITY...

Realigning Your Thoughts with Abundance 2.0

What would Abundance 2.0 look like in your life? Imagine waking up every day with the unshakeable belief that there is enough. Enough money, enough love, enough success. Picture making financial decisions from a place of trust and confidence rather than fear and doubt. Instead of being afraid to invest, you trust you're making wise choices. Instead of holding onto every dollar for fear of losing it, you let your money work for you because you believe there is more to where that came from.

When you operate on Abundance 2.0, you can be generous because you know generosity begets more abundance. You don't fret about what others are doing because there's no sense of competition—only collaboration. Scarcity says, "There's not enough for everyone, so I must fight for my share." Abundance says, "There's more than enough for us all, and my success adds to the collective prosperity."

Exercise: Writing New Code

Take a few minutes today and write a new set of affirmations—a new code—for your mental operating system. Keep them simple and direct, and make sure they resonate with you. Here are a few examples to get you started:

- "I am deserving of limitless wealth."
    - "Money flows to me in expected and unexpected ways."
    - "I have everything I need to be successful."
    - "The universe is abundant, and I actively participate in that abundance."

Write these affirmations down, or come up with your own. Repeat them daily. Use them like lines of code, entering them into your system until they run on autopilot.

Another exercise to try is a simple visualization practice. Spending five minutes each morning picturing your life as if Abundance 2.0 is fully installed. Imagine how different your day would be. Picture your interactions, your energy, and your attitude. Let those images sink in—they are seeds you plant for the future.

Upgrading Takes Time, But It's Worth It

Changing your mental operating system is not an overnight process. Scarcity 1.0 has been running for a long time, and upgrading it to Abundance 2.0 will take patience and consistency. There will be moments when your old coding re-emerges—when fear takes over, or a setback makes you question everything. That's okay. Every system has glitches. The key is to keep writing, visualizing, and believing in your new abundance script.

In this new Aquarian age, wealth is more than just a number in your bank account. It's about the fullness of your life, the opportunities you create, and the joy you spread. By upgrading your mindset, you're not just setting yourself up for financial gain—you're opening yourself to a life rich in every possible way. Start the upgrade today, and watch as your world upgrades as well.

Chapter 7: Energy Management - The New Time Management

Eckhart Tolle once said, "Time isn't precious at all because it is an illusion." And if time is an illusion, then managing it becomes a bit of a joke, doesn't it? You can't manage something that isn't real. But energy—energy is real. You can feel it when you have it, and you sure as hell feel it when you don't. So, instead of optimizing every hour of your day, it makes more sense to focus on managing what is tangible: your energy.

Imagine for a moment that you are a rechargeable battery. It is not some everlasting, superhuman battery. Still, a regular one—one that needs to be charged, wears down with use, and has limits. In this age, everyone seems obsessed with "maximizing time," like it's some linear thing that we can endlessly stretch out and fill with productivity. But time, as Tolle says, is an illusion. Our energy dictates what we do, how well we do it, and how much we enjoy it. It's not the minutes that matter; it's what you bring to those minutes.

The old model they used to sell us was all about fitting as much as possible into every hour. Wake up at five, work out, start emails by six, power through the morning, take a power lunch (not a real lunch, just a "power" one), and then keep going until the wheels fall off. That model was all about squeezing the juice out of time, thinking time was a limited resource. But here's the thing: you can have 24 hours in a day, and if you don't have the energy to live them well, they don't mean a thing. It's like having a car with a full gas tank but a dead battery—you're not going anywhere.

Knowing When to Recharge and Discharge

Think of your personal energy like a rechargeable battery. Every action you take, every task you perform, has an energy cost. Some tasks are energy-drainers—they take a lot out of you. It could be a high-stakes meeting, a complicated problem to solve, or just dealing with something emotionally taxing. Then there are energy-givers—the things that charge you up. It could be a walk in the park, a conversation with a good friend, or just a moment of silence with your favorite tea.

If you try to discharge all day without ever recharging, you'll end up with nothing. You'll feel exhausted, burnt out, and unable to give your best to anything. Most of us have experienced that: the sensation of being totally depleted, of having no juice left to power even the simplest of tasks. When you think of yourself as a battery, you begin to realize the importance of recharging as much as you do of discharging. Energy management is knowing when to expend energy and when to take a step back to recharge.

The goal isn't to keep your battery at 100% all the time—that's not realistic. Instead, the idea is to balance the charge and discharge cycles so that you don't find yourself running on empty. It's about becoming attuned to your personal rhythms—understanding when your energy is naturally high and when it needs replenishment. It's about moving through life in a more graceful dance rather than a frantic sprint.

CHAPTER 7: ENERGY MANAGEMENT - THE NEW TIME MANAGEMENT

The Peaks and Valleys of Your Day

Everyone has peaks and valleys when it comes to energy. Maybe you're a morning person—you wake up ready to take on the world. Or perhaps you don't fully wake up until lunchtime, and your afternoons are your powerhouse moments. The problem is that we often force ourselves into a schedule that doesn't honor these natural highs and lows. We're told to be "on" during certain hours and "off" during others without any regard for our internal energy states.

Instead of trying to power through your valleys, lean into them. Use those times for tasks that don't demand a lot of energy. Don't try to tackle your most important projects during your energy dips—save those for when you're at your peak. This isn't about being lazy; it's about being strategic. Why fight against your biology? You are not going to win anyway. When your energy is high, that's the time for creativity, problem-solving, and high-impact work. When it's low, that's the time for rest, reflection, and recharge.

If you've ever found yourself procrastinating on a big task, it's likely because you were trying to do it at a time when your energy wasn't aligned with the challenge. Imagine charging a phone with only 5% battery left while streaming video at full brightness. You're just asking for frustration. Instead, charge first—and then perform.

Energy Management and Happiness

Let's not forget that managing energy isn't just about productivity—it's also about happiness. Burnout happens when you're running on empty and keep trying to go further and faster. When you're mindful of your energy, you don't just become more productive; you become happier, more balanced, and more fulfilled. You stop seeing rest as "wasted time" and start seeing it as a crucial part of your success.

Our culture tends to glorify the hustle, celebrating those who put in endless hours. But the truth is, productivity without joy is empty. It's a race without a finish line. You don't win by doing the most; you win by having a life that feels full and purposeful. Managing your energy is how you get there.

Think about someone who always seems upbeat, who has that sparkle in their eye, no matter what's happening. They're not people who work themselves into the ground; they're people who know how to protect their energy. They work hard, but they also know when to step back, when to breathe, when to let themselves recharge. It's not magic—it's smart energy management.

Exercise: Track Your Energy Highs and Lows

For this week, log your energy levels throughout the day. Grab a notebook or use your phone—whatever works. Note when you feel most awake, alert, and ready to tackle big tasks. Also, note when you feel like you're dragging and when focusing feels like climbing uphill.

This isn't about micromanaging every moment—it's about noticing your own unique patterns. Once you have a week's worth of data, look for trends. Do you have a burst of energy at 10 a.m.? Does your energy dip around 3 p.m.? Use this information to plan your tasks more effectively. If you know you have an energy peak in the morning, that's the time for your most important work. If you tend to dip in the afternoon, maybe that's when you take a break, go for a walk, or at least do something that doesn't require intense focus.

The more you track and observe your energy patterns, the better you'll get at managing them. You'll find that, instead of constantly trying to squeeze every drop out of the clock, you're able to move with ease—like

CHAPTER 7: ENERGY MANAGEMENT - THE NEW TIME MANAGEMENT

that battery that knows precisely when to charge and when to power up. The end result? More productivity, more happiness, and, ultimately, a more abundant life.

Chapter 8: Authentic Value Creation - The Alchemy of Turning Skills Into Wealth

Albert Einstein once said, "Try not to become a man of success, but rather try to become a man of value." It's a beautiful sentiment, but in our world, the two often seem inseparable. We think of success as a measure of wealth—and wealth as a measure of value. But what if we flipped that perspective? What if the true path to wealth was to focus entirely on creating value and let the money be a natural byproduct?

Authentic value creation isn't about manipulating the market or finding the latest trend to exploit until it's dry. It's about tapping into your genuine abilities—your skills, your passions—and seeing how they can solve a problem, fill a gap, or make someone's life better. It's alchemy, in a sense. You take what you have, transform it into something more significant, and in doing so, create wealth for yourself and for others.

Turning Skills into Gold

Let's take another little story. It's about a young artist named Maya. Maya loved painting, but she had the stereotype of the "starving artist" down pat. She spent years trying to get galleries to exhibit her work, applying for residencies, and selling a painting here and there for a price

CHAPTER 8: AUTHENTIC VALUE CREATION - THE ALCHEMY OF TURNING...

that barely covered the materials. Her art was good—in fact, it was great. But her market? Well, it was non-existent.

One day, during a particularly frustrating period, she decided to create a portrait of her best friend's dog as a gift. It was playful and whimsical, different from the serious art she usually made. Her friend loved it, and she posted it on social media. Almost overnight, Maya started getting requests—people wanted portraits of their pets, their kids, and their grandmothers, all in the same lively, vibrant style. Maya had stumbled onto a niche that truly resonated.

Suddenly, she wasn't starving anymore. She was thriving. The value she provided—joyful, personalized art that captured something precious—was something people were willing, even eager, to pay for. She didn't compromise her skills; she found a unique way to apply them. That's authentic value creation. It's about meeting the market, not with a product that feels forced, but with something that only you can uniquely provide.

The Alchemy of Value

So what's the secret to this alchemy—this process of turning your skills into wealth? It starts with recognizing the difference between just being "good at something" and providing genuine value. Lots of people are good at lots of things. The magic happens when you find a way to use those abilities to solve a problem or fill a need in someone's life.

The marketplace is saturated with millions of generic offerings. But what it truly craves is authenticity—something unique, something real. Imagine your skills as ingredients: baking flour, sugar, butter, eggs. By themselves, they're fine. But when you combine them in exactly the right way, they transform into something far more valuable—a cake that people will pay for. That's the alchemy of authentic value creation.

It's taking the ingredients you already have and transforming them into something authentic that others need or desire.

The beauty of the Aquarian age is that people want connection, authenticity, creativity, and solutions that resonate on a truly personal level. No one wants cookie-cutter, mass-produced experiences anymore. This is why finding and creating genuine value is more important than ever. Your uniqueness is your advantage. The key is to look at your gifts and ask, "How can this make someone else's life better? How can it make a difference?"

The Curse of Comparison and Finding Your Niche

One of the biggest blocks to authentic value creation is comparison. The world is full of copies - and copies will never be great. We see others succeeding in their fields and think, "I need to do that." We try to copy their methods and follow their paths, hoping this will lead to the same pot of gold. But this never works because their value isn't our value.

Imagine you're an apple tree looking at a thriving orange grove. You might think, "People really seem to like oranges. Maybe I should start growing them." But an apple tree can't grow oranges—it can only produce apples. And those apples are incredibly valuable in the right market and with the right people.

To create real wealth, you have to stop focusing on what others are doing and start getting honest about what makes you unique. The moment you do, you'll find your niche. You'll find the people who want what only YOU can give. Like Maya, who discovered that her bright, playful style was perfect for pet portraits, you need to find where your gifts meet the needs of others. That's where the gold is.

CHAPTER 8: AUTHENTIC VALUE CREATION - THE ALCHEMY OF TURNING...

Bringing Value to Life: The Mindset Shift

Often, people think their talents are not enough. The thought of "Who would pay for this?" keeps many from even trying. But value isn't about grandiosity—it's about connection. Think about the last time you paid for something that brought you joy or made your life easier. It might have been a handmade candle, a home-cooked meal, or a book that spoke to your soul. The creators of those things probably wondered, at some point, if anyone would care. But the value was there. The connection was real.

The key to turning skills into wealth is to shift your mindset from "How can I be successful?" to "How can I provide value?" This changes everything. Instead of trying to fit into someone else's mold, you begin to see opportunities where your unique skills can shine. You stop trying to grow oranges and start tending to your apples.

Think about the people who are happiest in their work—those who seem to radiate enthusiasm and fulfillment. They aren't chasing the next big thing; they're doing what they do best in a way that others benefit from. They're solving problems, filling needs, and creating experiences that matter. And in return, they are rewarded—not just financially, but in knowing that their work makes a difference.

Exercise: Identify Your Skills and Their Value

Take a moment to think about three skills or talents you possess. Write them down. These could be anything—maybe you're great at organizing, maybe you have a knack for making people laugh, or maybe you're a natural at photography. Don't limit yourself by what you think is "valuable" right now—just focus on what you're good at.

Next, ask yourself, "How could these skills solve a problem or bring joy to others?" If you're great at organizing, maybe you could help overwhelmed people simplify their spaces. If you're funny, you could perhaps create content that helps people smile during tough times. If you're a photographer, maybe you could capture the special moments in people's lives in a way that they can cherish forever.

Finally, think about the niche where these skills could genuinely shine. Who are the people that need what you have? Start small, start simple, but start. Authentic value creation doesn't happen overnight, but when you find that sweet spot where your skills meet the needs of others, wealth follows. Real wealth—not just in your bank account, but in your heart as well.

The alchemy of turning skills into wealth is about seeing what's already within you and using it to serve others. It's about creating something genuine, something that adds value. You don't need to be everything to everyone—you just need to be authentically you and find the people who need exactly what you have to offer. That's where the magic is. That's how wealth is truly created.

Chapter 9: The Zen of Money - Balancing Attachment and Abundance

Wayne Dyer once said, "The secret of life is to be happy while you're working towards something." This is the heart of the Zen of money—the art of balancing desire and contentment. It sounds contradictory at first: how can you want more while also being satisfied with what you have? But therein lies the magic. The energy you bring to your financial journey has an enormous impact on what you attract, and often, being too attached to an outcome is precisely what keeps it from manifesting.

Imagine holding a handful of sand. If you squeeze your fist as hard as you can, clenching and clutching, the sand slips right through your fingers, leaving you with only a few stubborn grains. But if you relax your hand and hold it gently, the sand remains, resting easily in your palm.

Money works in much the same way. You lose your grip when you cling to it, obsessing over every dollar, worrying about where it will come from. The harder you cling, the more it seems to evade you. When you hold it lightly and approach it with both intention and trust, it appears to accumulate naturally.

The Power of Detachment

Detachment doesn't mean you stop caring about wealth or that you stop striving for it. It means you release the desperate energy that says, "I must have this, or I will be incomplete." Detachment means trusting that what is meant for you will come and that the journey to wealth is about more than the destination. You can still want something, even want it deeply, without being emotionally chained to it.

Consider this: when you're too focused on a particular outcome—say, making a specific amount of money by a certain date—it can create tension, anxiety, and a feeling of lack. You focus on what you don't have, which keeps you in a scarcity mindset. The universe, or your subconscious (whatever you want to call it), tends to respond to that energy with more scarcity. You're broadcasting lacks, and you end up attracting more of it.

Detachment is the art of knowing that your wealth will come but not being obsessed with exactly how or when. It's the belief that what you need is already on its way, and in the meantime, you are perfectly capable of enjoying the life you have right now.

Imagine you're a farmer. You plant seeds, you water them, and you trust that, in time, they will grow. You don't stand over them every minute of the day, demanding that they sprout immediately. You give them the space to grow. Your financial journey works the same way. You do the work but don't suffocate the process by constantly worrying about whether it will bear fruit.

CHAPTER 9: THE ZEN OF MONEY - BALANCING ATTACHMENT AND...

The Paradox of Wealth Attraction

Here's the paradox: the less you chase money, the more it comes to you. Wealth isn't about frantic pursuit. It's about aligning yourself with abundance and letting it flow to you. People who are desperate for money often repel it. They are normally the poorest. They make hasty decisions, act out of fear, and give off an energy that's rooted in anxiety. In contrast, those with a relaxed approach to money tend to attract it more easily. Why? Because they aren't vibrating on the frequency of desperation.

Picture two people walking on a beach, both trying to find seashells. One is rushing frantically, running back and forth, hunched over, grabbing at anything that looks like a shell. The other is walking calmly, enjoying the sun, glancing down occasionally. Who do you think finds the most beautiful shells? The one who is relaxed, open, and observant. Money flows the same way. You miss opportunities that could bring real wealth when you're constantly rushing after them.

Living With Enoughness

Living in the energy of "enoughness" means recognizing the wealth that already exists in your life. This doesn't mean settling or giving up on your dreams of more. It means acknowledging the abundance you already possess—whether it's the roof over your head, the food on your table, or the friends who support you. When you live in a state of gratitude for what you have, you open up space for more to flow in. Gratitude is a powerful attractor.

Think of it like a magnet. When you constantly lament what you lack, you become a magnet for more lack. When you focus on what you already have, appreciating even the smallest blessings, you become a magnet for more of that energy—more blessings, more abundance, more wealth. It's the difference between coming from a place of desperation versus a place of trust and joy.

The Balance of Action and Trust

Understand this - detachment isn't about inaction. You still need to show up, work towards your goals, and make some smart choices. But the trick is to balance that action with trust and using your intuition. You act from a place of joy, of creation, of contributing value to the world, rather than from fear or desperation. You trust that your efforts will bear fruit, even if it takes time.

A gardener doesn't just plant seeds and walk away forever—they water, they tend, but they also trust that growth is happening beneath the surface even when they can't see it. This is the Zen approach to wealth—to do the work but then release attachment to the outcome. The growth will come, but it doesn't need to be forced. In fact, the more you try to force it, the more likely you are to harm the process.

Exercise: The Money Meditation

Meditation is a powerful way to cultivate detachment, and abundance is through meditation. For this exercise, take 10 minutes out of your day to practice a "money meditation" focused on gratitude.

Find a quiet place where you won't be disturbed. Sit comfortably, close your eyes, and take a few deep breaths. Start by focusing on the things in your life that you are grateful for right now. It could be your health, your loved ones, your skills, or even the air you breathe. Allow yourself to feel that gratitude fully.

Now, shift your focus to the money you currently have—no matter how much or how little. Be grateful for it. Visualize it as energy, as something flowing in and out of your life, and know that more is on the way. You are simply a vessel for this energy, and it is limitless. There is no shortage, no need to cling. You are supported, and the wealth you need is always arriving exactly when it's meant to.

Repeat this meditation daily, even if only for a few minutes. Over time, it will help you cultivate a relaxed, trusting relationship with money—one that invites abundance rather than repels it.

Conclusion: Hold It Lightly

The Zen of money is about holding your financial dreams lightly, like that sand resting gently in your palm. You nurture them, you give them space, and you trust that, in time, they will come to fruition. Money is energy—it flows, it changes, and it responds to how we interact with it. The more we release our desperation, the more we align with abundance. The secret, then, is to be happy while you're working towards something. To live in the now, to appreciate what already is, and to trust that what's meant for you is on its way.

Chapter 10: Prosperity Through Collaboration - From Competition to Co-Creation

Helen Keller said, "Alone, we can do so little; together, we can do so much." In an era where competition has long been the default, it can be easy to think that the only path to success is to be better, faster, or smarter than everyone else. But in the Aquarian Age, the paradigm is shifting. The world is waking up to the power of collaboration, of creating something greater than the sum of its parts. And there lies the secret to true prosperity—not through competition but through co-creation.

Imagine a jazz band. Each musician is a master of their craft—the drummer keeps time with a steady, exciting rhythm, the saxophonist breathes life into the melody, and the bassist lays down the coolest groove. Each person knows their instrument intimately, but they aren't competing to see who can play the loudest or the fastest. They're collaborating, listening to each other, finding space within the music to add their own unique sound. When they come together, something magical happens. It's no longer about individual skill—it's about creating something that none of them could have done alone. That's the essence of collaboration.

The Aquarian Shift: From "Me" to "We"

The old world was built on competition. We were taught that in order to succeed, someone else must lose. Whether it's in business, sports, or even school, we were conditioned to believe that the world is a zero-sum game—that there's only so much success to go around. We watch TV programs where people are sent home – one by one. Just to end up with one – the best. But this mindset, rooted in scarcity, misses the bigger picture. True wealth, true innovation, and true progress come not from beating others but from building together.

In the Aquarian Age, collaboration is key. Think about some of the most impactful companies in the world today. Many of them started not by one genius working in isolation, but by groups of people coming together, sharing their talents, and co-creating something remarkable. Companies like Airbnb or Uber weren't just about individuals finding a way to dominate a market—they were about creating platforms where people could share resources, work together, and mutually benefit. These kinds of ventures thrive because they embrace the concept of abundance: the idea that there's enough success for everyone when we work together.

Collaboration isn't just about forming business partnerships, either. It's about the way we approach every part of our lives. It's about realizing that we are all part of an interconnected web. Your success doesn't detract from mine—in fact, it can enhance it. We all grow when we share our skills, knowledge, and energy. It's about moving from a "me-first" mentality to a "we-first" mentality.

Examples of Prosperity Through Co-Creation

There are countless examples of how collaboration leads to greater prosperity. Take, for instance, the world of open-source software. Projects like Linux and Wikipedia weren't built by one person, or even one company. They were built by countless individuals who believed in the power of sharing, pooling their knowledge and skills to create something that everyone could use and benefit from. These projects are living proof that collaboration can lead to incredible wealth—not necessarily in the form of money, but in the form of shared resources and knowledge that improve everyone's lives.

Or consider farmers who form cooperatives to share equipment and resources. Instead of each farmer struggling to afford expensive machinery alone, they pool their resources. This reduces their costs, improves their productivity, and strengthens their support for each other in times of need. One farmer's success becomes the success of the whole group, strengthening the community's prosperity.

Even in creative fields, collaboration is the secret sauce. Many of the most iconic films, albums, and art installations weren't the work of one singular genius, but of teams of creatives feeding off each other's energy and ideas. It's in the bouncing of ideas back and forth, in the blending of perspectives, that true magic happens. When we let go of the ego-driven need to do it all ourselves, we open up to the immense possibilities that come from working together.

Jazz Band Economics

Let's go back to that jazz band for a moment. Imagine if each band member decided they wanted to be the star—that they wanted the spotlight on them and only them. The music would turn into a chaotic mess—a cacophony of competing sounds, each one fighting to be heard over the others. The beauty of jazz, and the beauty of true collaboration, lies in knowing when to play and when to give others space to shine. It's about listening as much as it is about playing.

This is the essence of prosperity through collaboration. It's not about losing yourself or sacrificing your individuality—it's about contributing your unique gifts to the larger harmony. When everyone plays their part and brings their best without overshadowing others, the result is a symphony of abundance. Everyone benefits, everyone grows, and the collective creation is far greater than anything any one person could achieve alone.

Reaching Out and Building Together

It's easy to stay isolated. It's easy to think, "I must do this all by myself." Maybe it's pride, perhaps it's fear, or maybe it's just the way we've been taught. But the truth is, our most incredible opportunities often come when we step out of that mindset and reach out to others. Whether it's a business venture, a creative project, or even personal growth, the power of collaboration can take you further than you ever could go alone.

Think about the people in your life right now—friends, colleagues, acquaintances. Who could you partner with? Who has skills or resources that complement your own? Instead of seeing others as competition, start seeing them as potential partners. It could be as simple as sharing ideas, or it could be something bigger—like starting a joint venture, working on a creative project together, or even just supporting each other's growth.

Exercise: Reach Out for Collaboration

For this chapter's exercise, I want you to identify someone in your network—a friend, a colleague, or even someone you've only connected with online—and reach out to explore a potential collaboration. This doesn't have to be a major business endeavor. It could be as simple as co-hosting an event, sharing each other's work, or brainstorming ideas together.

Send them a message, and be open and honest about what you're looking for. Remember, collaboration is about creating something mutually beneficial, so think about how you can bring value to them as well. See where the conversation leads. Reaching out alone is a step towards breaking down the barriers of competition and moving into a space of co-creation.

The Collective Power of "We"

In the end, the path to prosperity isn't lonely. It's a journey that's richer and more rewarding when we walk it together. The Aquarian Age is calling us to let go of the outdated mindset that says we must compete, hoard, and dominate. It's inviting us to step into a new way of being—one where we uplift each other, share our gifts, and co-create something beautiful and abundant.

Just like the jazz band, each of us has our own unique part to play. Alone, our tune might be beautiful, but together, we can create a masterpiece. The key to prosperity is not in beating others on the way to the top—it's in helping each other rise and creating harmonies instead of solos. Collaboration is not just the future—it's the present. And the sooner we understand it, the sooner we all thrive.

Chapter 11: Emotional Wealth - Transforming Financial Anxiety

Søren Kierkegaard said, "Anxiety is the dizziness of freedom."

When it comes to money, anxiety often feels like dizziness—a swirling sensation that leaves us feeling unsteady, vulnerable, and out of control. But what if we could learn to steady ourselves? What if we could make our way through the storms of financial anxiety in a manner that allows us to grow instead of shrink? In this chapter, we'll investigate the relationship between emotions and economic well-being and learn to transform fear into a tool for emotional wealth.

The Weather of Your Emotions

Try to think of your emotions, like the weather. Sometimes, it's sunny and clear—everything feels stable, and the future seems bright. Other times, dark clouds roll in, and it feels like a storm is right on top of you, battering you from every angle. The key to emotional wealth is recognizing that these storms are just passing events; they don't define the landscape. Just because it's raining today doesn't mean it will be raining forever. Your financial anxiety, like the weather, is temporary—it's a cloud that will eventually pass.

But it can be hard to see beyond the next flash of lightning in the middle of the storm. Financial worries are deeply personal. They tap into some of our most primal fears—the fear of not being able to provide, of losing control, of not having enough. The irony is that, in our quest for financial security, we often create more emotional instability for ourselves. We get caught up in the storm, unable to see that the ground is still solid beneath the passing rain.

The Impact of Emotional Wealth on Financial Success

Emotional wealth isn't about ignoring your fears; it's about understanding them and putting them into perspective. Fear, after all, has a purpose. It's a signal that something needs attention. But when fear turns into chronic anxiety, it can become paralyzing. It can keep you from making wise financial choices, investing in yourself, and seizing opportunities. Emotional wealth is the ability to acknowledge that fear without letting it take the wheel.

Imagine a captain steering a ship through stormy waters. The anxiety is the storm, but the captain—that's you. The ship is more likely to capsize if the captain panics and starts making erratic movements. If the captain stays calm, keeps the eyes on the horizon, and adjusts course carefully, they can navigate through the worst of it. Emotional wealth is like that steady hand on the wheel. It doesn't mean the storm isn't happening—it means you're confident in your ability to get through it.

Tools for Managing Financial Anxiety

How do we start transforming financial anxiety into emotional wealth? Here are a few practical tools that can help:

1. **Reframe Your Thoughts:** Financial anxiety often stems from catastrophizing—imagining the worst-case scenarios over and over again. When you catch yourself in this loop, pause and ask yourself: What's the evidence for this belief? Could there possibly be another perspective? Often, our fears are based on assumptions rather than facts. By questioning these assumptions, you start to create a more balanced view.

2. **Gratitude Practice:** It might sound simple, but cultivating gratitude can have a profound impact on your financial well-being. Take time each day to write down three things you're grateful for—including financial blessings, no matter how small. Gratitude shifts your focus from scarcity to abundance, and when you're focused on abundance, you're more likely to make decisions from a place of confidence rather than fear.

3. **Mindful Breathing:** Anxiety lives in the body as much as it does in the mind. When you're feeling overwhelmed by financial stress, take a moment to breathe. Breathe in for four counts, hold for four, and breathe out for four. This helps activate your parasympathetic nervous system, calming your "fight or flight" response and allowing you to approach your finances with a clearer head.

4. **Release Attachment to Outcomes:** Just as we talked about in Chapter 9, one of the primary sources of financial anxiety is the obsession with controlling outcomes. You can make the best plan, follow all the proper steps, and still have unexpected things happen. Emotional wealth is about releasing that tight grip on outcomes and trusting in your own resilience. It's about knowing that you'll find a way through no matter what happens.

Facing the Worst-Case Scenario

A powerful exercise for transforming financial anxiety is facing the fear head-on. We often avoid thinking about our worst-case scenarios because they seem too terrifying to confront. Ironically, the act of looking directly at those fears can diminish their power.

Take a moment to write down one financial fear you have—something that's been nagging at the back of your mind. Now, take that fear and explore it fully. What's the absolute worst thing that could happen? What would you do in that situation? How would you survive? How would you rebuild?

You'll likely find that even your worst-case scenario has solutions. You might realize that, while uncomfortable, it wouldn't be the end of the world. You'd find a way through. And once you know that you have the inner strength to handle even the toughest challenges, the power that fear holds over you starts to diminish.

Emotional Wealth as a Foundation for Financial Growth

It's important to remember that emotional wealth isn't separate from financial wealth—it's the foundation of it. When you manage your emotions effectively, you make better decisions. You're more likely to take calculated risks, invest in your future, and pursue opportunities that align with your values and goals. Anxiety keeps you small; emotional wealth allows you to expand.

Think of your financial journey as a landscape. Sometimes, there will be storms—moments of uncertainty, unexpected expenses, market fluctuations. But beneath those storms, the landscape remains. The trees keep growing; the rivers keep flowing. Your emotional wealth is that landscape—stable, resilient, and always capable of renewal.

Financial anxiety might be a storm passing through, but it doesn't define who you are or where you're going. By learning to weather these storms with grace and perspective, you create a stable foundation for not just surviving but thriving.

Moving Forward

Transforming financial anxiety into emotional wealth is a journey—one that requires patience, self-compassion, and a willingness to face your fears. But when you shift your relationship with money, you'll find that the storms grow less frequent, the skies clearer, and the path forward more inviting. Remember, as I wrote at the beginning of this chapter, anxiety is the dizziness of freedom. It's a sign that you have choices, that you're stepping into the unknown. Fully embrace that dizziness, steady yourself, and keep moving forward. The landscape of your financial life is always capable of blossoming, no matter how heavy the clouds may seem.

Chapter 12: Creative Income Streams - Unlocking Your Inner Entrepreneur

"Don't put all your eggs in one basket." This old proverb is a piece of timeless financial wisdom that speaks directly to the heart of wealth creation in the Aquarian Age. Relying solely on one source of income—one basket—puts you at risk. If that basket tips over, the eggs crack, and you're left starting from scratch. Instead, imagine planting different seeds, each one yielding a new kind of fruit. In this chapter, we will explore how to cultivate a garden of financial abundance by leveraging your hobbies, skills, and creative endeavors to generate multiple income streams.

The Age of Multiple Income Streams

In the old economic paradigm, the goal was stability: get a good job, work your way up the ladder, and retire comfortably. That was the one basket. But today, the economy is shifting, and nothing is really stable anymore.

Jobs that once seemed stable are now uncertain, and relying on a single employer or income source can be very risky. The beauty of the Aquarian Age is that the tools of entrepreneurship—once available only to a select few—are now in everyone's hands. Anyone with a skill, a passion, or

CHAPTER 12: CREATIVE INCOME STREAMS - UNLOCKING YOUR INNER...

even just a spark of curiosity can turn that energy into income.

Think of your financial life as a garden. If you only plant one kind of seed, you're entirely reliant on that crop. If it fails, you're left with nothing. But if you plant many different types of seeds—some flowers, some vegetables, some herbs—you increase your chances of harvesting something throughout the year. If one crop fails, others will still thrive. This metaphorical garden can be cultivated using your skills, hobbies, and passions—each seed representing a potential income stream.

The Power of Hobbies and Passions

Most people think of income in terms of jobs and careers. But what about hobbies? What about those things you love to do in your spare time? What if they could be seeds for new income streams? Consider what you enjoy—maybe it's painting, playing music, cooking, gardening, writing, or photography. Each of these hobbies has the potential to become a source of income. It doesn't have to be complicated or overwhelming—you don't need to turn your life upside down to get started. It's about looking at what you already do and finding ways to share it with others.

Let's say you love baking. You could offer to bake for small events, start a blog or YouTube channel showcasing your favorite recipes, or sell baked goods at a local market. You could even create an online course teaching others how to make your signature desserts. Each of these approaches represents a different seed—some might grow fast, others slower, but they all contribute to your garden of abundance.

Or maybe you're into photography. With smartphones and social media, photography has never been more accessible. You could sell prints online, offer portrait sessions, teach others how to take better photos or license your images to websites and publications. Again, these are different seeds, each offering its own potential harvest.

The key is to see the value in what you're already doing. Too often, we underestimate our hobbies and passions. We think they're just for fun, just for us. But the world is full of people looking to learn, connect, and experience the things that come naturally to you. By sharing your passions, you not only enrich your own life but also create something of value for others—and that's where income streams begin.

Turning Skills Into Services

Another powerful way to create income streams is by leveraging your skills. Do you have a knack for writing, graphic design, coding, or public speaking? These are all skills that others are willing to pay for. In today's gig economy, you don't need to start a formal business or commit to a full-time venture. Instead, you can freelance on platforms like Fiverr, and Upwork, or even offer your services locally. Each freelance job you take on is another seed you plant—it's another step towards building multiple income streams.

Think about skills that might seem mundane but are incredibly valuable to someone else. Are you great at organizing? People need help with everything from decluttering their homes to streamlining their businesses. Are you a good listener? Life coaching or mentoring can be incredibly rewarding, both emotionally and financially. The skills that come naturally to you might be a lifeline to someone else—a way to solve a problem they don't know how to handle alone.

Experimenting With Different Seeds

The beauty of creating multiple income streams is that you don't have to get it all right from the beginning. It's about experimenting, planting different seeds, and seeing what grows. Maybe you start selling handmade jewelry and realize it's not for you. That's okay—you learned something. Meanwhile, your writing gig takes off, or your gardening YouTube channel gains followers. The point is to keep experimenting and to stay curious.

Remember, not every seed will grow into a massive tree—and that's perfectly fine. Some income streams might remain small, but collectively, they create a garden that flourishes in abundance. Even a little side income from a hobby or freelance project can contribute to your overall financial health, provide more security, and give you the freedom to explore your other passions.

It's also important to note that multiple income streams don't have to be entirely separate from each other—sometimes they can support one another. For instance, if you start a blog about painting, you could later develop an online course about painting techniques or sell your artwork directly to your readers. One seed can lead to another, creating a whole network of interlinked income opportunities.

Embracing the Entrepreneurial Mindset

At the heart of all of this is the entrepreneurial mindset—the belief that you have something of value to offer and the willingness to share it with the world, whether you think big or a bit smaller. Entrepreneurship isn't just about starting companies or creating products. It's about taking initiative, finding solutions, and recognizing that you have the power to shape your financial future. It's about viewing the world through the lens of possibility and abundance rather than limitation.

Entrepreneurs don't wait for opportunities; they create them. They look at the skills and resources they already have and ask, "How can I use this in a new way? How can I solve a problem or bring joy to others?" By unlocking your inner entrepreneur, you're allowing yourself to see the value in what you do and share it in a way that benefits you and the world.

Exercise: Brainstorm Your Creative Income Streams

For this chapter's exercise, I want you to brainstorm three potential creative income streams you could start this month. These could be based on hobbies, skills, or even just things you've always been curious about. Don't worry about making them perfect—just focus on generating ideas.

1. **Hobby-Based Income Stream:** Think of a hobby you love. How could you share it with others? Could you sell a product, create content, or teach a skill? Write down one idea for how this hobby could become an income stream.

2. **Skill-Based Income Stream:** Think of a skill you have—something you're good at or that people come to you for. Could you offer it as a service? Could you freelance, coach, or consult? Write down one idea for how to turn this skill into income.

3. **Experiment Income Stream:** Think of something you've always been curious about but haven't explored yet. Is there a way to turn that curiosity into an experiment that could generate income? Maybe it's creating digital content, making crafts, or learning a new skill that could be monetized. Write down one idea for an income experiment you could start.

The point of this exercise isn't to overwhelm yourself with too much, too soon. It's about planting seeds—about starting small, experimenting, and seeing what works. Over time, these seeds grow, and you'll find yourself with a garden of income streams that collectively bring you the security, freedom, and abundance you deserve.

Chapter 13: Ethical Wealth Building - Prosperity with Integrity

"Do the right thing. It will gratify some people and astonish the rest."
—Mark Twain

Ethical wealth building isn't just about how much money you can make; it's about how you make it and what you do with it once you have it. It's about ensuring that your path to prosperity not only enriches yourself but also leaves a positive impact on the world around you. In a society increasingly demanding accountability, transparency, and sustainability, building wealth ethically is a pathway to true, lasting prosperity—prosperity with integrity.

Ethical Practices and Conscious Capitalism

The concept of conscious capitalism has gained traction in recent years as people have begun to recognize that business can—and should—be a force for good. Conscious capitalism is about reimagining the purpose of business beyond the sole pursuit of profit. It's about creating value for all stakeholders—employees, customers, communities, and the environment—not just shareholders.

Take companies like Patagonia and Ben & Jerry's, for example. Both have made a commitment to use their businesses as a platform for positive change. Patagonia actively champions environmental conservation, using sustainable materials and encouraging customers to recycle or repair products instead of constantly buying new ones. Ben & Jerry's, meanwhile, has never shied away from using its brand to support social causes, including climate justice, fair trade, and racial equity. These companies prove that profitability doesn't have to come at the cost of ethics—that you can succeed in business while still making choices that benefit society.

Socially responsible businesses are a beacon of hope in a world where corporations are often vilified for exploiting people and resources. By investing in such companies or modeling your business practices after them, you are not only building wealth but also contributing to the well-being of the larger community. Ethical wealth building can include treating employees well, using environmentally friendly production methods, giving back to the community, and ensuring that your profits do not come at the expense of someone else's suffering.

Wealth as a Lighthouse

Think of wealth as a lighthouse. A lighthouse does not hoard its light; instead, it uses its brightness to guide others and lead them safely away from dangerous waters. Ethical wealth works the same way. It's not just about accumulating money for personal security or luxury—it's about using what you have to light the path for others, to share knowledge, opportunities, and resources that help uplift the lives of those around you.

Wealth built ethically has the power to influence and inspire. When people see successful individuals or businesses prospering through ethical practices, they are encouraged to do the same. You become a lighthouse in your community, showing that it's possible to achieve prosperity without compromising on your values, without taking shortcuts, and without exploiting others. You demonstrate that ethical wealth is not only possible but also sustainable and deeply rewarding.

The wealth you build with integrity isn't just for you. It serves a larger purpose, guiding others, supporting those in need, and contributing to positive social change. Ethical wealth building is about stewarding your resources, making decisions that reflect your values, and leading by example. It's about understanding that with wealth comes power, and with power comes responsibility. When you take on the responsibility of ethical wealth building, you add light to the world, showing others that it is possible to succeed while staying true to fairness, justice, and sustainability principles.

Examples of Ethical Wealth Building

Countless examples of individuals and organizations have successfully built wealth ethically. Consider Warby Parker, a company that set out to disrupt the eyeglass industry by providing affordable eyewear while giving back. For every pair of glasses sold, they distribute another pair to someone in need. This "buy one, give one" model is an example of a business that has built wealth by uplifting others.

Another example is The Body Shop, a pioneer in ethical consumerism. The company has always prioritized fair trade, cruelty-free testing, and environmental sustainability. Founder Anita Roddick believed that business could be a force for positive social and environmental change—a principle that has endured even as the company has grown and faced challenges.

These businesses are not just profit-generating machines; they are role models for ethical wealth-building. They show us that financial success and doing the right thing are not mutually exclusive. Instead, they are part of a cycle—doing good attracts loyal customers, builds a strong brand, and ultimately contributes to financial growth.

Exercise: Reflect and Improve

For this chapter's exercise, take some time to reflect on how your current income generation aligns with your values. Are you making money in a way that feels right to you? Are your investments and business practices aligned with the kind of world you want to help create?

Write down one change you could make to improve the alignment between your financial actions and your values. Perhaps it's moving your investments to a socially responsible fund, choosing to support businesses that have ethical labor practices, or even starting a community project that gives back meaningfully. The goal here is to bring greater alignment between how you build wealth and the positive impact you want to have in the world.

The Lasting Impact of Ethical Wealth

Building wealth ethically is not always the easiest path—there will be times when shortcuts or less scrupulous choices may seem tempting. But prosperity built with integrity is wealth that lasts. It's wealth that doesn't just enrich your bank account but also enriches your spirit, your community, and your legacy.

When you choose to build wealth ethically, you become part of a larger movement toward conscious capitalism and responsible prosperity. You become a lighthouse, guiding others toward a better way of doing business, creating abundance, and living. The wealth you create isn't just yours—it becomes a source of good in the world, a force that lifts others and leaves a lasting, positive impact.

Chapter 14: Aligning with Universal Cycles - Timing Your Investments

"To everything, there is a season." This quote from Ecclesiastes 3:1 speaks to a fundamental truth about life: everything moves in cycles. There is a time for sowing, a time for reaping, a time for resting, and a time for growth. Just as nature has its seasons, so does the finance world. Aligning your financial decisions with these universal cycles can be the difference between a barren field and a harvest overflowing with abundance. In this chapter, we'll explore the power of timing your investments in sync with the rhythms of the universe.

The Wisdom of Farmers

Imagine a farmer who plants his crops at the wrong time of year—in the dead of winter or the height of summer. No matter how good the soil is or how hard he works, the yield will be minimal. In contrast, a farmer who aligns with the natural rhythms—who plants in spring, nurtures through summer, and harvests in autumn—reaps the full potential of the earth. The farmer doesn't fight against the seasons; he moves with them, trusting that each phase has its purpose.

The same principles apply to investing and financial decisions. Just like nature, the economy has its seasons—periods of growth, decline, rest, and renewal. Recognizing these cycles and aligning your actions can help you maximize your gains and minimize your losses. When you invest at the right time, it's like planting seeds in fertile soil during spring—your chances of a bountiful harvest are significantly greater.

Economic and Market Cycles

One of the most powerful cycles to understand is the economic cycle. Economies move through phases: expansion, peak, contraction, and trough. During expansion, businesses grow, employment rises, and the stock market often sees substantial gains. This is akin to spring and summer—the time to plant, grow, and invest. But just as summer inevitably turns to autumn, economies, too, reach a peak and begin to contract. In these phases, it's wise to take stock of your investments—to consider harvesting what you've grown, or to prepare for the economic "winter" of a downturn.

This cycle repeats repeatedly, and while no one can predict the exact timing, understanding where we are in the cycle can help you make more informed decisions. Instead of panicking during a downturn, you can see it as an opportunity to buy lower-priced assets, much like planting seeds in winter that germinate when spring arrives. Aligning your financial moves with these cycles helps you take advantage of the natural ebb and flow of markets.

Seasonal Patterns and Investing

It's not only the economic cycle that can guide your investments—seasonal patterns also play a significant role. For instance, the stock market tends to perform differently in different seasons. Historically, the months of November through April have shown more substantial returns than the summer months. This phenomenon, often called the "Halloween Effect," suggests that certain times of the year are generally more favorable for investing.

Think of these seasonal patterns as micro-cycles within the larger economic rhythm. Understanding these smaller cycles can help you fine-tune your investments. You don't need to be a financial expert to benefit from this awareness—you just need to be mindful that markets, like nature, move through repeating rhythms. When you start to view your investments in this light, you become more patient and less reactive. Instead of panicking during downturns, you understand that winter is just one part of the cycle—a necessary phase that makes way for spring.

Personal Cycles and Intuition

Beyond economic and seasonal cycles, it's also essential to consider your own personal cycles. Each of us has periods when we feel more energized, focused, and ready to take risks—and times when we feel more cautious, and reflective, and need to conserve our resources. Aligning your financial decisions with your personal cycles means listening to your intuition and recognizing when it's the right time for you to act.

For example, you might feel an internal "spring" when you're excited about a new business idea or an investment opportunity. It's during these moments that your intuition and energy align with action. In contrast, during your personal "autumn," you might feel the urge to pull back, reassess, and harvest the gains of your past actions. Honoring these internal rhythms can help you stay aligned with what's best for your overall financial journey.

Moving with the Flow

Aligning with universal cycles isn't about trying to time the market perfectly. No one can predict precisely when the market will rise or fall, just as no one can predict the precise day spring will arrive. Instead, it's about moving with the flow of these cycles rather than trying to resist them. It's about recognizing that there are times for aggressive action, times for cautious planning, and times for rest.

One of the biggest mistakes investors make is acting out of sync with the natural rhythms of the market. During periods of economic contraction, fear can drive people to sell investments at a loss, locking in their losses rather than riding out the cycle. But just as a farmer wouldn't destroy his crops at the first sign of cold weather, investors should remember that downturns are a natural part of the financial ecosystem. Winter always turns into spring—and when it does, those who have remained patient and aligned are best positioned to thrive.

Exercise: Research and Plan Your Next Move

For this chapter's exercise, take some time to research one market cycle relevant to your finances. It could be the broader economic cycle, seasonal trends in the stock market, or even real estate cycles. Understanding where we currently are within that cycle can help you make a more informed decision about your next financial move.

Once you've done your research, write down one action you could take that aligns with this cycle. It might be investing in an asset that's currently undervalued, setting aside cash in preparation for an upcoming downturn, or holding off on a purchase until the cycle turns more favorable. The key is to take a step that aligns with the rhythm of the market—to act like a wise farmer, planting at the right time to reap a

CHAPTER 14: ALIGNING WITH UNIVERSAL CYCLES - TIMING YOUR...

bountiful harvest later on.

Chapter 15: Sustainable Wealth Practices - Building Lasting Prosperity

"We do not inherit the earth from our ancestors; we borrow it from our children." This Native American proverb reminds us that our choices today don't just affect us—they ripple out, shaping the future we leave for future generations.

When it comes to wealth, true prosperity is not measured only by the numbers in your bank account; it's measured by the impact you create, both for your own future and for the world around you. Sustainable wealth is about creating prosperity that endures—financial security that doesn't deplete the earth or the well-being of others. This chapter will explore building wealth that lasts and contributes to a healthier, more balanced world.

Building a Strong Foundation

Imagine you are building a house where you plan to live for the rest of your life, a place that could shelter not only you but your children and their children. Would you build it on shaky ground with weak materials to save a little money or time? Or would you lay a strong foundation, ensuring every brick, beam, and nail is placed with care?

Sustainable wealth is like that well-built house. It requires a solid foundation—wise financial choices, ethical investments, and practices that respect both the earth and the people on it. It's not about getting rich as quickly as possible or accumulating wealth without regard for its impact. It's about creating a legacy of prosperity that endures and benefits others, long after you're gone. A house built on a weak foundation will crumble in a storm, but a home built with care will stand tall through the changing seasons. The same is true for your wealth—it's only as strong as the foundation on which it's built.

Wealth That Works for the Planet

The importance of environmentally sustainable practices cannot be overstated. We live on a planet with finite resources, and our financial decisions directly impact the environment. Investing in companies that prioritize sustainable energy, ethical sourcing, and responsible manufacturing is one way to ensure that your wealth contributes to a healthier world.

Consider this: every dollar you invest is a vote for the kind of world you want to create. By investing in businesses that prioritize renewable energy, reduce waste, and care for their workers, you're contributing to an economy that benefits both people and the planet. Just like a house that's built to be energy-efficient, with solar panels and water-saving systems, your wealth can be designed to be in harmony with the earth. It's more than just minimizing harm—it's about actively contributing to the environment's well-being.

The beauty of sustainable wealth is that it's also financially smart. Companies that prioritize sustainability are often better prepared to navigate future challenges. As resources become scarcer and the effects of climate change become even more visible, businesses that operate sustainably are more likely to thrive. By aligning your investments with sustainability, you're not just doing what's right but also setting yourself up for long-term financial growth.

Social Sustainability: Wealth That Lifts Others

Sustainable wealth is also about social responsibility. It's about recognizing that true prosperity isn't built by stepping on others but by lifting them up. This means considering how your wealth-building practices impact other people—from the workers who produce the goods you buy to the communities affected by the businesses you support.

Fairtrade, ethical sourcing and investments in community development are all ways to ensure that your wealth supports others in meaningful ways. Think about the people involved in every step of the products you buy and the services you use. Are they paid fairly? Are they treated with respect? When you choose to support businesses that prioritize social responsibility, you help create a system in which wealth is shared more equitably, where opportunities are available to more people, and where prosperity lifts entire communities.

Like a well-built house that provides shelter for everyone inside, sustainable wealth is inclusive. It doesn't just serve your interests; it serves the interests of others, contributing to a better quality of life for all. When you think about wealth as a way to create a positive impact, you move beyond the narrow view of personal gain and start seeing the broader possibilities—how your prosperity can contribute to a better world.

Moving from Unsustainable to Sustainable Practices

Wealth built unsustainably is like a house that looks beautiful on the outside but has been constructed with cheap materials. It might stand for a while, but eventually, it will start to show its flaws—cracks in the foundation and leaks in the roof. Unsustainable wealth is built on practices that exploit resources, people, or both. It prioritizes short-term gain over long-term health; ultimately, it can't last.

To build lasting prosperity, it's essential to move away from unsustainable practices. This might mean changing how you invest—looking for funds focusing on sustainability or divesting from companies that harm the environment or exploit workers. It might mean reconsidering how you spend your money, choosing quality over quantity, or supporting businesses that align with your values.

Small changes can have a significant impact. For example, consider making your business practices more sustainable if you're an entrepreneur. Could you reduce waste, ethically source materials, or create a more inclusive workplace? If you're an investor, consider funds prioritizing ESG (Environmental, Social, Governance) criteria. If you're a consumer, think about the life cycle of the products you buy—where they come from, how they're made, and where they end up.

Exercise: Identify and Shift One Unsustainable Habit

For this chapter's exercise, take some time to identify one unsustainable habit in your finances. This could be anything from investing in companies that don't align with your values, to spending money on products that harm the environment. Once you've identified this habit, write down one specific change you can make to shift it toward sustainability.

Maybe it's choosing to invest in a green energy fund, or deciding to buy fewer but higher-quality products that last longer. Perhaps it's choosing to support local businesses that give back to their communities. The key is to take one step, however small, toward making your wealth-building practices more sustainable. Over time, these small changes add up, creating a foundation for prosperity that lasts for you and future generations.

Building Wealth That Endures

Sustainable wealth is about creating something that lasts—not just here today and gone tomorrow, but that continues to grow and support others long into the future. It's about building a house with a strong foundation—one that shelters not only you but also the generations that follow. By aligning your wealth practices with sustainability, you're not just building financial security but a legacy of positive impact.

The choices you make today shape the world of tomorrow. Committing to sustainable wealth ensures that your prosperity is built on a foundation of integrity, care, and foresight. You become a steward of both your own future and the future of the world we all share—and that is the true essence of lasting prosperity.

Chapter 16: Generosity as a Wealth Accelerator - The Power of Giving

Pablo Picasso once said, "The meaning of life is to find your gift. The purpose of life is to give it away." In a culture that often equates wealth with accumulation, it can seem counterintuitive to say that giving is actually a key to growing wealth. But the truth is, generosity is one of the most powerful accelerators of abundance you can ever tap into. By giving back, we create a flow—a movement of energy that enriches not only those who receive but also ourselves.

Imagine wealth as a river. When it flows, it brings life, nourishes the land, and keeps everything around it vibrant. But if that river becomes blocked, it becomes stagnant if the water stops moving. Life around it wilts, and what was once fresh and thriving starts to decay. Wealth works in much the same way. It must flow to stay fresh and abundant. Hoarding wealth, holding it tightly in fear of losing it, creates stagnation—just like the river that no longer moves. But when you allow wealth to flow and share it freely, you keep the energy moving, and the abundance multiplies.

The Law of Circulation

The concept of giving as a means of growing wealth is rooted in what some call the "law of circulation." This law suggests that everything in the universe, including wealth, operates in cycles. When you give freely, you allow more to come into your life. Generosity opens up a channel, creating a natural balance of receiving and giving. It is through this cycle that abundance continues to grow.

Think about the wealthiest and most fulfilled people you know. Chances are, they give back in some significant way. They donate to causes they care about, mentor others, or contribute to their communities. It's not just about the amount of money they give—it's about the intention behind it. They understand that by letting their wealth flow outward, they keep it circulating, attracting even more prosperity.

Generosity isn't about emptying your pockets without thinking of yourself; it's about realizing that the more you give, the more you invite abundance to flow into your life. When you shift your mindset from "How can I keep everything I have?" to "How can I use what I have to benefit others?" you trigger an energetic shift that begins to attract new opportunities, connections, and wealth.

Giving from the Heart

Generosity isn't just about money. It's about giving your time, talents, attention, and care. You might not always be able to provide financially, but that doesn't mean you can't be generous. Perhaps you have a skill that could help someone, or maybe you can offer your time to support a cause you care about. Generosity is about opening up, sharing what you have, and trusting that your giving creates ripples that will eventually return to you.

The beauty of giving is that it shifts your focus from lack to abundance. When you give, you affirm to yourself and the universe that you have enough. You say, "I am already abundant and have more than enough to share." This is a powerful statement—not just of wealth but of trust. It's trust in yourself, trust in the flow of life, and trust that there is always more to come.

You begin to see the world differently when you give from a place of joy, without expecting anything in return. You notice opportunities you might have missed before, attract people who share your values, and feel a deeper connection to the abundance already around you. Generosity becomes a wealth accelerator because it aligns you with the very essence of abundance—flow.

The Flow of Wealth as a River

Let's return to the metaphor of a river. A river that flows freely brings life to everything around it. Fish thrive, plants grow, and animals come to drink from its waters. The river doesn't hoard its water; it shares it freely, and in doing so, it becomes a source of life for everything around it. This is how wealth should work in our lives. When we allow our wealth to flow—whether it's financial wealth, the wealth of our time, or the wealth of our talents—we create a thriving environment for ourselves and those around us.

If you think of wealth as something to be protected and hidden away, you end up creating a dam. Sure, the water accumulates for a time, but eventually, it stagnates. The energy is blocked, and instead of flowing freely, it begins to decay. But when you choose generosity, you remove the dam and allow the water to nourish everything around it. You become a source of life, joy, and abundance for others, and in doing so, you bring more wealth into your own life.

Generosity isn't about giving until you're empty but creating a steady flow. It's about realizing that what you give will come back to you in some form, perhaps in ways you can't even anticipate. When you let go of the fear of losing and embrace the flow of giving, you become part of something larger, something that moves in harmony with the natural rhythms of the universe.

Acts of Generosity: Practical and Meaningful

The idea of giving might sound abstract, but it's essential to make it practical. Start small. Maybe it's donating a portion of your income to a cause that resonates with you. Perhaps it's spending an afternoon volunteering at a local charity. Maybe it's using your skills to help someone who could benefit from your expertise. The key is finding a form of generosity that feels meaningful to you and aligns with your values.

The power of giving is that it doesn't just change the world around you—it changes you. It cultivates a mindset of abundance, of knowing that there is always enough. It reminds you that wealth is not just about what you accumulate, but about the positive impact you create with what you have.

Exercise: Plan an Act of Generosity

For this chapter's exercise, I want you to plan one act of generosity that aligns with your financial means and feels meaningful to you. This doesn't need to be a grand gesture; it could be something as simple as buying lunch for someone who needs it, donating to a charity, or spending time helping a friend with a project. The key is to do it with a spirit of giving, without expecting anything in return.

Write down what you plan to do and how you think it might impact both you and the recipient. Reflect on how this act of giving makes you feel—before, during, and after. Notice if it shifts your perspective on wealth, abundance, and generosity.

The Ripple Effect of Generosity

Generosity creates ripples. When you give, you inspire others to give. Your generosity becomes a catalyst, touching the lives of people you may never meet. It accelerates wealth, not just financially, but in the richness of experience, connection, and community. When you become a river flowing freely, you nourish yourself and the world around you.

The power of giving is profound. It is a reminder that we are all connected, and that true wealth is not measured by what we keep but by what we share. By embracing generosity, you invite abundance into your life in deeper, more meaningful, and more fulfilling ways. You become part of the flow, and in that flow, you find that wealth is not just something you have—it's something you are.

Chapter 17: The Creative Economy - Abundance Through Innovation

Albert Einstein said, "Creativity is intelligence having fun." There has never been a better time for your creativity to take center stage as a true driver of wealth and abundance. The traditional boundaries of work and value creation are shifting. More than ever, we are seeing the rise of a new kind of economy—one driven by innovation, artistry, and unique contributions. This is the creative economy, redefining what wealth means in the 21st century.

Imagine an artist standing before a blank canvas, armed with various colors on their palette. Each color represents a different skill, talent, or idea. The artist mixes these colors, trying new combinations and applying brushstrokes in various ways, creating something uniquely their own. This is the essence of the creative economy. Wealth is no longer just about accumulating money; it is about weaving together your talents, passions, and innovations to create something meaningful and impactful.

The Rise of the Creative Economy

The creative economy is one where value is generated through originality, artistic expression, and innovative thinking. It thrives on the principle that everyone has something unique to offer—an idea, a perspective, a skill—that, when expressed, contributes to the richness of the world. In this economy, the value isn't just in the product itself; it's in the creativity behind it, the story it tells, and the community it builds.

Think about platforms like Etsy, YouTube, or Patreon. These are all examples of how the creative economy is flourishing today. Artists, content creators, musicians, and makers of all kinds are leveraging technology to reach audiences directly, bypassing traditional gatekeepers. These platforms have transformed the economic landscape, allowing people to monetize their creativity in ways that simply weren't available a generation ago.

Take, for example, a ceramic artist who sells her handmade pottery on Etsy. She's not just selling a bowl; she's sharing a piece of herself, a glimpse into her process, dedication, and love for the craft. Buyers aren't just purchasing an item—they're buying into a story, an experience, and a connection. In the creative economy, value is more than just functionality; it's about beauty, emotion, and meaning.

This shift towards creativity as a source of wealth is liberating. It means wealth is no longer reserved for those who fit into traditional corporate roles or climb established career ladders. Instead, anyone with a creative spark—whether in art, writing, music, problem-solving, or anything else—can harness that creativity to generate value and, by extension, wealth.

Your Palette of Skills

The artist's palette is a powerful metaphor for this new way of creating wealth. Each of us has unique colors—skills, experiences, passions, and ideas—that we can use to create our masterpiece. Maybe you're a teacher who loves photography, or maybe you're a software developer with a passion for music. The creative economy encourages us to combine these colors in new ways, to blend different parts of ourselves to create something that stands out.

Think of someone like Elon Musk. He didn't just stick to one color on the palette. He blended engineering, business, innovation, and an unyielding curiosity about the future to create something that pushes boundaries. Or consider someone like Beyoncé, who combines her vocal talent, storytelling ability, understanding of culture, and business acumen to build an empire. They bring value not from sticking to one skill but from blending multiple talents into something extraordinary.

You don't need to be famous or exceptionally well-known to do this. In your own way, you can start painting your masterpiece by taking stock of what you have—your colors—and thinking about how they can come together to create something of value. Maybe it's a blog that combines your love of travel with your passion for cooking, or a workshop that teaches people how to build their own furniture. The key is to look at what you love, what you're good at, and what the world needs, then find the intersections.

Innovation as a Wealth Driver

The beauty of the creative economy is that it rewards innovation. Innovation is about doing something differently, seeing an opportunity where others see a problem, and thinking outside the traditional structures that have defined work and wealth. It doesn't have to involve creating the next big tech product; it can be as simple as finding a new way to reach people, a unique twist on an existing idea, or a fresh approach to a well-worn craft.

Consider the rise of digital content creators—people who, from their bedrooms, have managed to create careers by sharing their thoughts, talents, and experiences online. They didn't wait for someone to give them permission to start. They used the tools available, embraced their uniqueness, and found ways to share their gifts with the world. The creative economy is all about leveraging the resources at your disposal to innovate, connect, and contribute.

This new economy also reminds us that creativity and wealth are not mutually exclusive. There is a false belief that artists must struggle and that creativity is somehow less valuable than more "practical" skills. The creative economy challenges this idea by showing that there is immense value in originality, beauty, and storytelling. When paired with innovation and action, creativity becomes not just a means of expression but a powerful driver of financial abundance.

Exercise: Brainstorm Creative Solutions

For this chapter's exercise, I want you to spend 30 minutes brainstorming creative solutions to a financial challenge you are currently facing. Maybe you're looking for a way to earn extra income, or perhaps you want to save more effectively for a future goal. Whatever it is, approach it with the mindset of an artist standing in front of a blank canvas.

Write down all your ideas, no matter how unconventional they might seem. Could you leverage a hobby to create an extra income stream? Could you offer a service in your community that others might need?

This exercise aims to push beyond the obvious and see your financial situation as a canvas on which you can paint new possibilities. Let your creativity and your intelligence have fun with it.

The Power of the Creative Economy

The creative economy is a testament to the power of human ingenuity. It's proof that wealth isn't just about what you have; it's about what you can create. By tapping into your unique skills and combining them in innovative ways, you can generate abundance, not just for yourself but also for those around you.

In the creative economy, the possibilities are endless because each person's palette is different. There is no one right way to create wealth—there is only your way, the way that blends your colors into a masterpiece that is uniquely yours. The key is to embrace your creativity, trust your ability to innovate, and remember that abundance is not reserved for a select few. It's available to all of us when we are willing to create, connect, and share our gifts with the world.

Chapter 18: Financial Resilience - Weathering Economic Storms

"Smooth seas do not make skillful sailors." This African proverb is a reminder that true strength is forged in times of challenge.

The same is true for financial resilience. We often talk about wealth in terms of growth and abundance, but equally important is the ability to weather the storms—the economic downturns, the unexpected expenses, and the fluctuations that are a natural part of life. In this chapter, we will explore how to build financial resilience so that you can sail confidently through calm waters and the inevitable storms.

Navigating the Sea of Finances

Try to see your financial life as a ship at sea. There are days when the water is smooth, the sky is clear, and you can see your destination on the horizon. But the ocean is unpredictable, and there will also be days when the sky darkens, the wind picks up, and waves crash against the bow. The key to reaching your destination is not to avoid the storms altogether, but to be prepared to navigate them skillfully and confidently.

Financial resilience is about preparing your ship for all conditions. It's about ensuring you have the proper safety equipment on board—the savings, the insurance, the flexibility—that will allow you to weather any storm without capsizing. It's about knowing how to adjust your sails when the wind changes and stay calm even when the waves feel overwhelming.

Building Your Financial Safety Nets

The first step to financial resilience is building a solid safety net. This includes creating an emergency fund that can cover unexpected expenses, such as medical bills, car repairs, or periods of unemployment. An emergency fund is like having a lifeboat—something to keep you afloat when the waters get rough. It provides peace of mind, knowing you have a cushion to fall back on when the unexpected happens.

Start by setting a goal for your emergency fund. Ideally, you should aim for three to six months' worth of living expenses. If that sounds daunting, don't be discouraged. The key is to start small and build consistently. Setting aside a little each week adds up over time, and every bit you save brings you closer to financial security.

Beyond an emergency fund, consider other safety nets like health, home, life, and even disability insurance. These tools help protect you from financial devastation in the face of unpredictable events. Just as a ship is equipped with life vests and flotation devices, having the right insurance means you're prepared if things go awry.

Adapting with Agility

Economic storms can take many forms—recessions, job losses, and market crashes. The key to resilience is agility. Just like a skilled sailor adjusts the sails to catch the wind or avoid a coming typhoon, financial resilience involves making changes when circumstances shift.

One of the best ways to stay agile is to diversify your income streams. When your income comes from one source, like a single job, you are vulnerable if that source dries up. Just as a ship with multiple sails can adjust more quickly to changing winds, having more than one income stream gives you flexibility. This might mean developing a side business, investing in different assets, or finding freelance opportunities. The creative economy we discussed in the last chapter is an excellent example of creating diverse income streams that can carry you through times of uncertainty.

Another aspect of agility is monitoring spending closely. When economic uncertainty looms, it's time to reassess your budget. Are there areas where you can cut back? Could subscriptions or habits be adjusted to free up more resources? This isn't about living in scarcity—it's about using foresight to ensure your ship stays light and agile, ready to navigate any obstacle.

The Importance of Foresight

Foresight is about thinking ahead and anticipating both opportunities and challenges before they arrive. A good sailor doesn't set sail without checking the weather forecast, and a financially resilient person doesn't go through life without planning for the future. This means setting financial goals, understanding your risk tolerance, and making decisions today that position you well for tomorrow.

Investing is one area where foresight plays a significant role. During periods of economic uncertainty, the stock market can fluctuate wildly. It's tempting to react emotionally by selling investments when prices drop or jumping on risky opportunities out of fear. But a resilient investor understands that storms are part of the journey. Instead of panicking, they stay the course, trust their plan, and look for opportunities others might overlook in times of fear.

Having a long-term financial plan helps provide direction even when things seem uncertain. It's like having a map that shows your destination, even if the waves are tossing your ship around in the short term. By staying focused on your long-term goals, you can weather the storms without losing sight of where you're headed.

Exercise: Strengthen Your Financial Safety Net

For this chapter's exercise, take a few minutes to review your current savings. Do you have an emergency fund? Is it enough to cover three to six months of your essential expenses? If not, create a plan to bolster your emergency fund. Set a realistic savings goal and determine how much you can set aside each month to reach it.

Next, review your insurance coverage. Do you have the proper protections for your life, health, and assets? Consider where you might need additional coverage or where you could make adjustments to better protect yourself from financial storms.

Finally, think about how you could make your financial ship more agile. Can you diversify your income or reduce your spending to be better prepared for changing circumstances? Write down one or two specific actions to build resilience in your finances.

Sailing Toward Your Financial Goals

Financial resilience is not about avoiding every storm—it's about being prepared to face them. It's about building a solid foundation, equipping yourself with the right tools, and staying flexible in the face

CHAPTER 18: FINANCIAL RESILIENCE - WEATHERING ECONOMIC...

of uncertainty. Just as a skilled sailor knows how to navigate both calm seas and turbulent waters, a financially resilient person knows how to thrive in times of prosperity and adapt in times of challenge.

You create a financial life that can weather any storm by building your financial safety nets, staying agile, and using foresight. You become the captain of your own ship, confident that no matter what the ocean throws your way, you have the skills and tools to reach your destination safely. And as you do, you'll find that the journey itself—the calm days, the stormy nights, the moments of triumph and challenge—becomes an integral part of your story of prosperity.

Chapter 19: Aligning Wealth with Purpose - Prosperity as a Life Mission

Friedrich Nietzsche said, "He who has a why to live can bear almost any how."

This quote speaks to the power of purpose—of having a driving reason behind everything we do. When it comes to wealth, aligning our financial goals with a higher purpose turns the pursuit of prosperity into something meaningful. It transforms wealth from mere numbers in an account into a tool for living out your mission and creating a lasting impact. This chapter will explore how aligning wealth with purpose can guide you to a more fulfilling life.

Purpose as Your Compass

See yourself standing at a crossroads, looking at a map with countless roads leading in different directions. Some roads seem promising, others daunting, and without a clear sense of direction, it's easy to feel overwhelmed. Imagine you have a compass—a tool that always points you toward your true north. It doesn't matter how confusing the roads are; you will always have a direction. That compass is your purpose, guiding every financial decision, and ensuring that your actions align with what truly matters to you.

CHAPTER 19: ALIGNING WEALTH WITH PURPOSE - PROSPERITY AS A...

Wealth without purpose is like a ship lost at sea without a compass—it drifts wherever the tides take it, always at the mercy of external forces. In contrast, wealth aligned with a mission becomes directed, intentional, and powerful. It moves with purpose, aiming towards a destination beyond personal gain. It's not just about having more; it's about having more so that you can do more, give more, and be more in the world.

The Why Behind Wealth

Too often, the pursuit of wealth is approached as an end in itself. We set financial goals—saving a certain amount, buying a particular house, achieving a certain income—without really questioning why these goals matter. But wealth, in and of itself, is empty without a purpose to fill it. What makes wealth meaningful is what you do with it, and how it helps you live a life aligned with your values, passions, and mission.

Take, for example, someone whose mission is to help underserved communities get access to education. For this person, wealth becomes a means to that end. Every financial decision—whether it's saving, investing, or donating—is made with the mission in mind. Instead of just amassing money for its own sake, this individual builds wealth to expand their ability to make an impact. The financial decisions are not random or purely profit-driven; they are part of a larger plan, a life mission that brings deep fulfillment.

When you understand your "why," you give direction to your "how." Instead of chasing wealth for the sake of luxury or status, you pursue it as a way to support your highest values and to make a difference in the areas that matter most to you. Whether that's providing for your family, supporting your community, or contributing to global causes, having a clear purpose transforms the pursuit of wealth into a meaningful journey.

The Fulfillment of Purpose-Driven Wealth

There's a profound difference between accumulating money for the sake of it and using money to fulfill a purpose. The former can feel like an endless cycle—no matter how much you accumulate, there's always more to want, achieve, and chase. The latter, however, brings a sense of fulfillment and satisfaction because each dollar has meaning. When your wealth is tied to a mission, the act of earning, saving, and investing becomes fulfilling in itself, because it's all contributing to something greater than you.

Consider again that metaphor of a compass. A compass doesn't care about the specifics of the journey—whether you're climbing a mountain, walking through a forest, or crossing a desert. It simply points you in the direction of your goal. When you use your purpose as your compass, it doesn't matter what specific challenges arise in your financial journey. Whether the market takes a downturn or you have to adjust your plan, your purpose keeps you on course. It provides the "why" to help you navigate any "how."

Purpose and Abundance

Aligning your wealth with your purpose also cultivates a mindset of abundance. When your financial goals are driven by a mission, you begin to see wealth not just as something to possess but as something to be used, shared, and used to create a positive impact. This perspective shifts you from a scarcity mindset—worrying about having enough—to an abundance mindset, focused on what you can create and contribute.

Abundance is not just about how much money you have; it's about how much good you can do with what you have. The person who uses their wealth to fund a cause they care deeply about is living abundantly, regardless of how their net worth compares to others. Purpose-driven wealth is inherently abundant because it's rooted in contribution. The more you give, the more you feel fulfilled, and the more wealth seems to flow into your life, because you are using it to serve something meaningful.

Exercise: Discovering Your Life Mission

For this chapter's exercise, take some time to reflect on your life mission. What is it that brings you the most fulfillment? What causes are you passionate about? What impact do you want to have on the world? Write down your life mission as clearly as you can.

Next, brainstorm ways that your financial actions can support this mission. How can your wealth—whether it's what you have now or what you're working towards—be used to further your mission? Could you allocate part of your income to support a cause you care about? Could you invest in projects or businesses that align with your values? Could you build your career or business around something contributing to your mission?

Write down as many ideas as you can, and then choose one that you can take action on in the near future.

The True Power of Wealth

The wealth that is aligned with purpose is powerful. It grows not just in numbers but in impact. When your financial journey is guided by a compass of purpose, you know that no matter what happens, you are moving in the right direction. Your wealth becomes a reflection of your values, a tool for fulfilling your mission, and a source of deep satisfaction.

The pursuit of wealth is not just about achieving security or comfort—it's about creating the means to live your life mission fully. By aligning your wealth with your purpose, you turn prosperity into something much more than a personal achievement. You create a legacy, a positive impact that can endure long after you're gone. In doing so, you fulfill your financial goals and the deeper desires that drive you, creating a life of true meaning and abundance.

Chapter 20: Generational Wealth - Leaving a Legacy

"A society grows great when old men plant trees whose shade they know they shall never sit in."

This Greek proverb speaks to the profound importance of thinking beyond ourselves—planting seeds today that will grow into a better future for those who come after us. When we talk about generational wealth, it's not just about passing down money or assets; it's about leaving a legacy of values, opportunities, and a foundation upon which future generations can build.

Planting Trees for Tomorrow

Imagine standing in a field, holding a young sapling in your hand. You know that planting this tree today will not give you immediate shade. It will not bear fruit for you tomorrow. But you plant it anyway, knowing that one day, it will grow tall and strong. It will provide shade and nourishment for those who come after you—your children, their children, and countless others. This is the essence of generational wealth: planting something today that will benefit others in ways that extend far beyond your own lifetime.

Creating generational wealth is about building something that endures.

It's about providing the financial resources that your children and grandchildren might need and instilling the values, wisdom, and habits that will help them make the most of those resources. It's about creating a foundation that allows future generations to thrive—not just financially, but emotionally, intellectually, and spiritually.

Financial Wealth That Endures

Financial wealth is a significant part of leaving a legacy. This doesn't necessarily mean amassing enormous wealth; it means making thoughtful decisions today that provide stability and opportunity for the next generation. This could be in the form of investments, property, or savings plans that grow over time, or it could be as simple as teaching your children about money management, the value of saving, and the power of intelligent investing.

One of the key elements of building generational wealth is ensuring it's protected and appropriately managed. Estate planning, trusts, and wills are all tools that can help ensure that the assets you accumulate are passed on smoothly and responsibly. It's like building a fence around that tree you planted—ensuring that what you've nurtured isn't trampled or misused.

Beyond leaving behind financial assets, think about what you want those assets to represent. Money, in and of itself, is neutral. It's how we use it, and the intentions behind it, that give it meaning. The wealth you leave can enable future generations to pursue education, create opportunities for themselves, and live lives full of purpose and possibility. It's about providing a stepping stone that helps them go further than you could, just as a tree provides a home for countless creatures that might never know who planted it.

CHAPTER 20: GENERATIONAL WEALTH - LEAVING A LEGACY

Your Values as Part of Your Legacy

Generational wealth is not just financial—it's also about passing down values, knowledge, and traditions. What beliefs and practices have guided you on your journey to prosperity? What lessons have you learned that you wish to share with your children and grandchildren? These intangible assets can be even more valuable than money, because they provide the wisdom needed to make the most of any material inheritance.

Consider the value of perseverance. Perhaps your own financial journey wasn't easy. Maybe you faced setbacks, challenges, and moments of doubt, but you pushed through. Sharing these stories with your children helps them understand that wealth is not just handed down—it's earned, often with hard work and resilience. When they hear your stories, they inherit more than assets; they inherit the mindset needed to maintain and grow those assets.

Another value to consider is generosity. As we discussed in the chapter on giving, wealth is most fulfilling when it's used to uplift others. By modeling generosity, you pass down a spirit of contribution—showing that wealth is not just for personal comfort, but for making a positive difference in the world. This, too, becomes part of your legacy, and it helps future generations use their resources wisely and compassionately.

Planting for Future Growth

Think of building generational wealth as planting an orchard rather than a single tree. Each tree represents a different aspect of your legacy—financial stability, values, opportunities, and lessons. As the trees grow, they form a resilient and interconnected forest, providing not just for one generation, but for many. The orchard becomes a thriving ecosystem, where each generation tends to the trees, plants new ones, and enjoys the fruit of their collective labor.

It's important to remember that generational wealth doesn't always consist of large amounts of money. It can be knowledge, a network of supportive relationships, or a passion for learning and creativity. The goal is not just to pass down wealth but also the ability to create wealth, make wise decisions, and live with purpose. When we plant these seeds, we invest in our descendants' strength and resilience.

Exercise: Start Your Legacy Plan

For this chapter's exercise, take some time to start a legacy plan. Begin by defining one value or asset you wish to pass on to the next generation. This could be a financial asset, like an investment or a savings account, or a value, like the importance of hard work, the power of kindness, or the value of continuous learning.

Write down how you plan to pass this asset or value on. If it's a financial asset, consider how you will ensure it is managed properly. If it's a value, consider the conversations you can have or the traditions you can establish to instill this value in your children or grandchildren. The key is to be intentional—to plant your tree with care, knowing that the shade it provides will one day comfort and protect those who come after you.

Leaving a Legacy That Matters

Generational wealth is about more than leaving behind money. It's about leaving behind opportunities, lessons, and a solid foundation that future generations can build upon. It is about planting seeds today that will grow into something beautiful, providing value far beyond your own lifetime.

The true power of wealth lies not in what it can do for us individually, but in what it can enable us to do for others—especially those who come after us. By aligning your financial actions to create a lasting impact, you ensure that your legacy is one of growth, resilience, and hope. You plant trees, not for yourself, but for the future—a future that will remember you not just for the wealth you left, but for the values, the opportunities, and the vision you nurtured.

Conclusion: Claiming Your Birthright of Abundance

As we reach the end of this journey, it's time to step back and look at wealth in all its forms. True wealth is not just limited to the digits in a bank account, the possessions we accumulate, or the titles we earn. It is multidimensional, stretching beyond the financial to encompass emotional well-being, meaningful relationships, spiritual fulfillment, and personal freedom. Real wealth is about the richness of experiences, the joy of giving, the empowerment of living aligned with one's values, and the satisfaction of a purpose-driven life.

In each chapter, we have explored different facets of wealth and how to unlock your full potential to create a life of abundance. We have looked at cultivating intuition, reprogramming scarcity beliefs, managing energy, creating authentic value, building ethical wealth, and leaving a lasting legacy, among many other powerful lessons. What emerges from all this is a vision of prosperity that is available to each of us if we are willing to see beyond the traditional definitions of wealth and take on a broader, more holistic understanding of what it means to live abundantly.

Abundance is your birthright. It is not reserved for the few or the fortunate—it is available to all who are willing to open their hearts and minds to the infinite possibilities that life holds. It is not something that is granted to you from the outside; it is a state of being that begins within. It starts with seeing yourself as deserving, capable, and connected to a limitless source of potential. It is about knowing that you have the power to create value, not just for yourself but for others, and that in doing so, you tap into the true essence of prosperity.

Taking Action Now

The time to claim your abundance is now. We are moving into the Aquarian Age—a time characterized by innovation, collaboration, and consciousness. The energies of this new era call us to move away from the outdated paradigms of competition, scarcity, and fear and to implement a new way of being that celebrates creativity, connection, and generosity. Aligning with these energies requires action, a willingness to step into the unknown, and the courage to redefine what wealth means for ourselves and our world.

Waiting for the perfect moment to take action is a trap that keeps many people stuck. The ideal moment is an illusion—the truth is that each moment holds within it the potential for transformation. Your life is happening now, and the choices you make today will shape the course of your future. Every decision you make to live more abundantly, to act with integrity, to share your gifts, and to align your wealth with purpose, adds to the momentum of your prosperity and helps build a world where abundance is the norm.

Aligning with the Aquarian Energies

The Aquarian Age brings with it a shift in consciousness. It makes us move from individualism to interconnectedness, from hoarding to sharing, from fear-based survival to love-based creation. It asks us to take responsibility not only for our own well-being but for the well-being of others and the planet as a whole. Claiming your abundance is not just about personal gain—it's about stepping into your role as a creator, a contributor, and a guide for others.

You are part of this shift. By choosing to create wealth consciously, ethically, and generously, you become a beacon of the new paradigm—a model of what is possible when we align our actions with our highest values and embrace the truth that there is enough for everyone. When you claim your abundance, you are not taking from someone else; you are creating value that did not exist before, adding to humanity's collective wealth.

A Call to Action

As you close this book, I invite you to take what you have learned and put it into action. Wealth is not a static goal—it is a dynamic journey. It is not something that just happens to you; it is something you create, nurture, and share. Embrace the exercises, the insights, and the challenges presented in these pages, and let them guide you toward a life of true prosperity.

Remember, abundance is not just about what you have—it's about who you become. It's about your choices, the people you uplift, the values you embody, and the love you share. It is about stepping into your full potential and creating a life that is rich in every sense of the word.

The journey to abundance is not always easy, but it is always worthwhile. It requires you to let go of old beliefs, face your fears, and trust in your own capacity to create and contribute. It asks you to see beyond the limitations of the past and embrace the limitless possibilities of the present. It challenges you to grow, stretch, and become the person you were always meant to be.

So, claim your birthright of abundance. Step into the Aquarian energies of innovation, collaboration, and purpose. Use your wealth—whatever form it takes—to make the world a better place. And remember, the time is now. Your life is happening now. The seeds of abundance are already within you, waiting to be nurtured and grown into something beautiful.

Take the leap. Trust in your journey. And live abundantly.

Epilogue: The Ripple Effect of Your Wealth

"Be the change you wish to see in the world." Mahatma Gandhi's words serve as a powerful reminder of the influence each of us can have.

When we think about wealth, it's easy to see it as personal—something that impacts only our lives and our immediate circle. However, wealth, when created ethically and with purpose, has a ripple effect that extends far beyond the individual. Your wealth, choices, and actions have the potential to uplift not only you but also your family, your community, and, ultimately, the world.

Imagine throwing a stone into a still pond. The ripples begin small, radiating out from the point of impact, growing wider and wider until they touch the edges of the pond. Your actions—especially the way you create and use your wealth—are like that stone. Each decision you make creates ripples that influence not only your life but also the lives of those around you. By choosing to build wealth with integrity, aligning your financial goals with your highest values, and using your resources to contribute to the greater good, you create ripples of positivity, inspiration, and change.

When you build wealth ethically, you become a way-shower of a new paradigm—one where prosperity is not built on exploitation but on empowerment; not on greed, but on generosity; not on fear, but on purpose. You show others that it is possible to thrive financially while remaining true to your values. You become an example of what is possible when abundance is approached with consciousness and care.

These ripples extend to your family. When you teach your children about financial literacy, about the value of giving back, and about aligning money with purpose, you are planting seeds that will grow for generations. You are giving them the tools not just to manage money, but to use it as a means of creating a fulfilling and meaningful life. Your wealth becomes a source of opportunities for those who come after you, enabling them to reach new heights and make their own contributions to the world.

The ripple effect of your wealth also extends to your community. When you support local businesses, invest in causes that uplift others, create jobs, or share your resources with those in need, you strengthen the fabric of your community. You contribute to an ecosystem of growth, support, and possibility. Imagine a community where each person takes steps to uplift others, where each individual's prosperity contributes to collective well-being. This is the power of conscious wealth, and it starts with each one of us.

On a broader scale, the choices you make with your wealth contribute to the global shift that is already underway. We are moving into an era where people are demanding transparency, sustainability, and fairness. By choosing to invest in companies that prioritize ethical practices and support initiatives that promote equality and environmental stewardship, you

are helping to shape a future where wealth is synonymous with positive impact. You are part of a collective movement towards a more equitable and compassionate world.

But the ripple effect isn't just about financial contributions. It's also about the energy and example you bring to those around you. When you live abundantly, when you embrace both prosperity and generosity, you inspire others to do the same. Your courage to pursue your purpose, your willingness to take risks, and your commitment to using wealth for good

CONCLUSION: CLAIMING YOUR BIRTHRIGHT OF ABUNDANCE

all serve as a beacon for others who are seeking a new way forward. You show them that there is another way—a way to succeed that honors the well-being of all.

Being a way-shower of conscious wealth is about embodying the change you wish to see. It's about demonstrating that success doesn't have to come at the expense of others—that it can, in fact, be a powerful force for uplifting everyone. It's about embracing the truth that your wealth is not just for you, but is also a tool for building a better world.

As you move forward from this book, remember that the ripples you create are not limited by time or distance. Every action you take, every choice you make in alignment with your values, adds to the wave of positive change that is reshaping our world. By choosing to live abundantly, ethically, and purposefully, you are contributing to a legacy of prosperity that benefits not only your life but the lives of countless others.

Claim your birthright of abundance, not just as a means of personal comfort, but as a means of creating a ripple effect of goodness, growth, and transformation. Be the change. Use your wealth, your talents, and your resources to leave the world better than you found it.

The ripples you create today will grow into waves of positive impact, reaching far beyond what you can see—touching lives, shaping futures, and building a foundation for a world defined by abundance, compassion, and purpose.

Thank you for reading this book

Please give Your Honest Review.

Thank you for joining the journey to discover wealth in a new way! If this book has brought you fresh insights, a new perspective, or simply a moment of inspiration, please consider leaving an honest review. Your feedback not only helps others decide if this book is right for them but also helps us reach more people who are ready to explore wealth in the Aquarian Age.

Your experience matters, and we'd love to hear it!

Continue Your Journey with Lucidism and the principles you have read in the book.

Thank you for reading! If Get Rich the New Way inspired you, more awaits you.

Visit lucidism.org and motivatrz.com to discover my other books and resources for living a truly lucid life. You'll find many more articles and free guided meditations to enhance the book's effect there.

Lucidism.org/bookbonus

Motivatrz.com/bookbonus

Sign up for our newsletter to stay updated on new books, insightful articles, and exclusive content.

Also, check out my YouTube channel, @Lucidism-Unfiltered, and my podcast, which has the same name (where you find your podcasts). We have unfiltered conversations on wealth, freedom, and personal growth.
    Join our community—let's make the journey toward freedom, purpose, and abundance together!

About the Author

Leonhart Lowell Laponnel is a Danish-born visionary and the creator of Lucidism (Life philosophy) and the Lucidism Global Initiative (LGI)—a transformative political movement built on the principles of personal freedom, authenticity, and spiritual growth. Rooted in a lifelong quest to break free from limiting beliefs and societal constraints, Leonhart developed Lucidism as a pathway to empower individuals to live fully and freely.

A deeper purpose beyond material success has always driven a former corporate leader, Leonhart. His journey from business management to spiritual leadership reflects his relentless commitment to creating a world where people are free to be their truest selves without fear of judgment or repression. Lucidism encourages individuals to question conventional norms, redefine success, and embrace life without boundaries.

At the heart of Leonhart's philosophy is the belief that freedom is a birthright. Under his guidance, Lucidism has become a sanctuary for free spirits, visionaries, and change-makers seeking a life of autonomy, purpose, and joy.

Through the Lucidism Global Initiative, he has created a movement that celebrates all identities and expressions, envisioning a world where each person can contribute to a collective evolution of freedom and possibility.

Leonhart invites you to join him on this journey, to discover the true essence of freedom, and to live a life that is authentically and unapologetically your own.

You can connect with me on:
- https://lucidism.org
- https://x.com/luciddhism
- https://www.facebook.com/luciddhism
- https://lgigov.org
- https://www.linkedin.com/in/laponnel

Subscribe to my newsletter:
- https://lucidism.org

www.ingramcontent.com/pod-product-compliance
Lightning Source LLC
Chambersburg PA
CBHW070235220526
45465CB00004B/1427